WARS AND BATTLES

UNTERNEHMEN MERKU[illegible]

José Antonio Alcaide

Artworks:
Luis Fresno Crespo
Juan Carlos Ciordia
Julio López Caeiro

AF EDITIONS

(Bundesarchiv 183-L19019).

INTRODUCTION

The Second World War was the most significant confrontation of the 20th Century. In fact, and for many of the followers of the N.S.D.A.P. (*Nationalsozialistische Deutsche Arbeiterpartei* or National Socialist German Worker's Party), was no more than a continuation of the First Great War, that was postponed with the Allied German Armistice and the Treaty of Versailles. However, this second part of the Great War of 1914-1918 had different political causes and above all, a different development and key figures to the previous.

With respect to the strategy and military tactics, it did not at all resemble that which had been developed over the previous twenty years. Although initially the Allies placed their bets on a war of positions, as they had done in the previous campaign of 1914-1918, this gamble was already quite behind the times compared with the innovations that the Germans were about to develop on the battlefield. The inertia instead of movement and the strong works and defensive fortifications that the Allies placed on the terrain were easily overcome by the new German concepts: Speed, moving firepower with aerial support and, above all, the flexibility that was provided by the new weapons and equipment in the hands of young soldiers, capable of adapting technological advances to the world of war and that would change the face of battle.

The *Luftwaffe* and its *Oberkommando der Luftwaffe* (high command of the German Air Force) provided a new concept in aviation and its use on campaign, with the inclusion of aerial infantry units, which, among other innovations incorporated the use of parachutes to transport the attack troops to the battlefield. This concept was to revolutionise the tactics, enabling a new type of attack to be carried out, "vertical envelopment". This enabled highly operative elite units to be situated behind enemy lines and attack specific objectives, for example, in order to open up a path that would facilitate the rapid advance of the armoured units towards their target. It was certainly a revolution in the art of war.

Erroneous conclusions were drawn from the airborne attack on the Belgian fort Eben Emael, which later proved disastrous for the attack on Crete. (Bundesarchiv 146-1971-011-31).

The *Fallschirmjäger* who obtained such a resounding success at Eben Emael posed on the 12th May 1940 for the photographer Büttner. (Bundesarchiv 146-1971-011-27).

However, like all progress, it was made in the form of small operations followed by analysing the results. The first of these operations were conducted in Scandinavia, the Netherlands and Belgium and were successful. Nevertheless, this very success, due to its novelty, occulted several setbacks that could occur afterwards.

During the first moments, the parachute attack doctrine provided these lightly armed fighters with the means of facilitating their mobility and the effect of surprise. The lack of reaction of the garrison defending Eben Emael and other places led to the consolidation of the error. It was necessary for "Operation Mercury" to take place, with its high mortality rate, in order to detect the great problem: The parachutists were too lightly armed, which meant that if they met with strong resistance, they were easily annihilated. Despite the lessons that could have been learned from "Operation Mercury", Hitler did not really understand what the problem was (the insufficient firing power) and thinking that the airborne attacks were simply too exposed, he decided to abolish the large paratrooper interventions, relegating these troops to elite infantry units. On the other side, the Allies only captured part of the message, as they reinforced their own airborne operations, resolving the problem of inadequate fire power by providing the airborne units with powerful weaponry. However, they ignored the other lesson: That the operations had to be planned with good information. When nothing is known about the place and defences of the target to be attacked, disaster can strike, as happened in Operation *«Market Garden»*. This paratrooper action was a resounding failure in which three divisions and two independent paratrooper brigades were annihilated in a question of hours. According to some authors, it was due to an Intelligence failure, although it was later discovered that in fact, Field Marshall Bernard Law Montgomery, First Viscount Montgomery of El-Alamein ("Monty" to the Allies), scorned the information provided by aerial photos that located vehicles of an armoured division in the jumping area. In fact, there were two armoured S.S. divisions (*9.-SS-Panzer-División «Hohenstaufen»* and *10.-SS-Panzer-Division «Frundsberg»*) which were reorganising there. Furthermore, the 3.

Fallschirnjäger Division was also stationed there as well as various small Wehrmacht units. The carpet of paratroopers fell directly on them in an attempt to capture the only two passable roads which crossed the Netherlands and headed for the heart of Germany.

Nowadays, paratrooper units are usually the elite units of any army and are trained and treating accordingly, but they are never happily exposed without having carefully prepared their actions. Intelligence is fundamental and the loss of men should be avoided whenever possible. Nowadays, fewer men are available for the action and it is very important to suffer few losses, as these men may be irreplaceable.

Notes important to this work

Several days before the end of the Second World War and with the Soviets at the gates of Berlin, several events occurred that are significant for discovering the "real history" of what had been happening during those years. The Nazi leaders decided to eliminate the huge volume of archives accumulated during the years in which Germany was under their control. On some occasions, this was achieved with greater success than on others.

Concretely, during the last days of April 1945, the *Reichminister der Luftfahrt and Oberbefehlshaber der Luftwaffe* (Minister of Aviation and Commander in Chief of the Air Force), Generalfeldmarschall Hermann Wilhelm Göring personally ordered for his departmental archives to be burnt. Luckily, there was not enough time for the action to be completed, and hence today, we are able to study the very complete reports on the Eastern Front, the most modern of the archives, while the oldest archives, such as those of the «Legion Condor» have literally disappeared. Many others vanished amidst the smoke and ash of the bonfires established by Herman Göring, which has resulted in large gaps in the military history of those years.

As far as this work is concerned, something very similar occurred with the general history of the *Luftwaffe*, as the greater part of the original documents were lost or destroyed. Contrary to general history, the later documents on this action are the most scarce and unknown, while the preparation of the operation and the first forty-eight hours of the attack are the easiest to describe in detail. There are various different versions, as the few existing documents have been compiled, studied and classified in different archives and by very different scholars of the theme, who by treating them in very diverse ways, have also obtained different results and sometimes drawn mistaken and even contradictory conclusions.

Another significant problem is that of the language and its translations. The original reports on *Unternehmen Merkur* are found in German and English and some are also in Greek, though these are a minority. The Germans had translated into their language Greek names and terms with Greek phonetics and writing. The English did the same thing, but with very different results. The outcome of the studies and the passage of time has brought these results to third languages, with new adaptations, phonetics and writing, which has resulted in numerous problems with the localisation of places and their real names.

Thus, different names for the same place appear, such as: Maleme, also called Chania or Canea, etc..., as well as the repetition of the same name for two different places: The town of Perivolia is a good example of which there are two, one next to Chania and the other next to Rethymno. In addition to this, some places and locations have changed their name since the World War. All of this has led us to reconsider the terminology of people and places. Current and above all direct translations from Greek to Spanish have been sought. To this end, we have used the terminology translated by the Department of Greek Tourism, perhaps the most appropriate given the circumstances and opportunity. Furthermore, we have tried to specify the names of doubtful places or duplicated names whenever this has been possible. We hope that the readers accept this rectification of the names that appear in other works, that we have found impossible to locate on the terrain, because the second or third transcription from Greek to English, to German, to finally reach the Spanish language has deviated the recognition of the real name of the place.

Among the *Fallschirmjäger* who were dropped during the attack on Crete, was the well-known boxer Max Schmeling, world heavyweight champion in 1930 and winner against the mythical Joe Louis in the famous fight on the 19th June 1936. (Bundesarchiv 146-1971-115-04).

CHAPTER I

When Adolf Hitler Pölzl, *Führer und Reichskanzler der Dritte Reich* (leader and chancellor of the Third Germanic Empire) conquered the greater part of the European continent between 1939 and 1941, the small island of Crete became a vital element in controlling the Eastern Mediterranean. For the United Kingdom, which was practically alone in North East Europe, surrounded by sea and at the same time protected by it, it was very important to maintain open its lines of communication with the colonies, as they supplied the mother country with all its needs. The Suez Canal and Gibraltar were the keys to the Mediterranean, but the route between the two points was too long and it was necessary to rely on several supporting ports and airports at the entrances to the Mediterranean. Malta, Crete and indirectly, Cyprus provided these provisioning points and also the aerial control that would enable the maritime routes to supply England.

Between 1940 and 1941, after having concluded that attacking the United Kingdom of Great Britain had become momentarily impossible, Adolf Hitler's strategy was gradually changed in favour of shutting away the indomitable island as much as possible. The headquarters of the *Führer* and the *Oberkommando der Wehrmacht* (Supreme Commander of the German Army) had planned several options, such as Operation *«Felix»*, Order Number 18 of the Führer's Headquarters, for the attack and control of Gibraltar. The rest of the priority objectives were to be ordered afterwards, such as the attacks on Malta, Crete and lastly Cyprus, as well as the conquest of North Africa from Italian Libya; all this in order to close the Mediterranean to the British Armed Forces. These actions would result in the supply distances from India and Australia being greatly enlarged, thus weakening British resistance. However, a series of events entered into the game of international diplomacy. Field Marshal Francisco Franco Bahamonde (Spanish Head of State) did not facilitate the development of Operation *«Felix»*. In fact, Hitler investigated the possibility of invading Spain, in spite of the Spanish friendship with the *Reich*, because curiously, the only Spanish monarchist and friend of the Allies was its Head of State: a real problem for the interests of the Reich. On the other hand, the apparent harmony of the German-Soviet Non-aggression Pact was just that, apparent, as it was only being maintained as a result of common interests. Once the signatories confronted each another, they headed hurriedly towards a brutal confrontation. In fact, at the start of *Unternehmen «Barbarrossa»*, Hitler's posture was to isolate Great Britain from its Empire as much as possible, as the Soviet Union was beginning to shape up as one of her future supporters. Hitler ordered for a new order to be prepared, which was emitted on the 18th December 1940, being Order Number 21. The Order defined the attack on the Soviet Union and fixed the attack for a date no later than the 27th May 1941. Meanwhile, the operations of the Italian Prime Minister, Benito Amilcare Andrea Mussolini, *il Duce* and the Italian Army in the Balkans and North Africa were having disastrous effects on the interests of the Axis.

The attack on Greece was finally made by Italy on the 15th October 1940. In the Venice Palace in Rome, Mussolini, Cíano, Badoglio, Soddu, Jiacomoni, Roatta and Visconti Prasca met together, that is, the fascist leaders of the time. In the meeting, a document (an ultimatum) was prepared for the Greek government. It was delivered by the Italian Ambassador, Emanuele Grazzi, to the Greek Prime Minister, General Ioannis Metaxas on the 28th October 1940 at three o'clock in the morning. After its delivery, three hours of grace were granted for a reply. General Metaxas replied with a single word: *Oxi* ("no" in Greek), which was to give rise to the future public holiday "Oxi Day". Metaxas only made one comment in French while reading the document: "*Alors, c'est la guerre*" (then it's war).

At six o'clock in the morning on the 28th October 1940, the Italian Army invaded Greece from Albania. Initially, it was easily predictable; the progression through Greek territory was quick and effective. But the Greeks initiated a reaction that firstly stopped the Italians on the 4th November and then managed to reintegrate the conquest forces behind their departure lines by the 12th November and even siege the Albanian city of Coritsa on the 22nd November. All of this resulted in the loss of almost 20% of the Italian troops. Meanwhile, in the other countries comprising the Balkans, diverse political events were taking place that were to influence Hitler's future options. In Yugoslavia, the young

Italian motorized troops (bersaglieri) ready to penetrate Greek territory from their bases in Albania. (Bundesarchiv F016230-0009a).

These same troops, during the initial rapid advance. (Bundesarchiv 122-FI16228-16a).

king Peter II, Prince Pavel (Paul), the king's uncle exercised power. The politicians running the country at the time were: Dragiša Cvetković, the president of the Royal Government and Dr. Vladko Maček, president of the Croatian Peasants Party (HSS). Prince Pavel was subjected to all kinds of pressure to make his country enter into one of the alliances possible at the time. However, the pressures of the Axis were the most effective. Firstly, there was a meeting in Berchtesgaden between the Yugoslav Minister for Foreign Affairs and Hitler, which ended in frugal commitment. Afterwards, and in accordance with the negative evolution of the Italian invasion of Greece, other confrontations took place, in which the consolidation of the Trilateral Pact gained more and more weight. Romania, Bulgaria, Hungary and Albania joined the pact, which left Yugoslavia surrounded by allies and sympathisers of the Italian–German Axis. Once again, Hitler met with Prince Pavel on the 5th March 1941, eventually giving him an ultimatum on the 19th March. It was unusually effective, because in less than forty-eight hours, the Yugoslavs entered into the German orbit. The Regent suffered immediately, with a coup d'etat on the 25th March. It was led by General Dušan T. Simovic and British diplomacy was possibly behind this action. Forty-eight hours later, on the 27th March, Hitler (in the midst of an outbreak of rage), ordered the elaboration of Order Number 25, which began with the following sentence by the Führer: "*The military revolt in Yugoslavia has changed the political situation in the Balkans. Yugoslavia, still declaring loyalty and respect for the Trilateral Pact, must be considered as an enemy and should be defeated as soon as possible.*" According to the order, Marshal List and his 12. Armee would invade Yugoslavia. On the 30th March, the order of operations was approved and on the 6th April, the action began under the command of Spoje. Meanwhile, Simovic ordered the Regent into exile, adopted a closer posture towards the Soviet Union and allowed himself to be influenced by the British. When the German attack became imminent, he tried to calm Hitler down by adhering to the Trilateral Pact, but it was too late. The Yugoslavs surrendered on the 17th April: The invasion had lasted eleven days.

After their surrender, the Yugoslav soldiers lay down their arms under the gaze of the German soldiers. (Bundesarchiv 75-36-24).

After signing the surrender, high-ranking officers of the Yugoslav Army were transferred to Berlin as prisoners. (Bundesarchiv 751-16-23).

The Führer's other problem in the Balkans was Greece. The solution came together with that of Yugoslavia. Since the Italian invasion, many things had happened Greece. In the first place, it must be acknowledged that the myth that Hitler was unaware of Mussoli's idea of invading Greece was false, as we will shortly demonstrate in another work. All the authors cite Hitler's rage at the resulting situation, but his anger was not because Mussolini had acted on his own initiative, but rather because the attack (which fitted perfectly with the plan as a whole), was a disaster from the first moment. The appropriate reaction of General Papagos, who in just seven days had stopped the advance of Mussolini's troops and had forced them to retreat, had raised doubts about the effectiveness of the Italian Army. Hitler needed to do something to play to the gallery that would strengthen the Italian position and also provide confidence to the troops. He decided to help Mussolini out of the stalemate in which he found himself, while he acted diplomatically on Yugoslavia, also in the dual political and military direction. To these ends, German diplomacy began to pressure the Greek dictator, General Ioannis Metaxas. The Greek general and dictator, of fascist ideology, had assumed power on the 13th April 1936, after having been named as prime minister by King George II, faced with the political chaos that existed in Greece. In spite of his fascist ideals, Metaxas believed in an alliance with the British, who were, according to him, the natural allies of Greece. And with this strange ideological baggage, he governed the country. He created *"Oxi Day"* (No Day), proclaiming the fight against Mussolini, Italy and their interference in Greece. This nationalist spur led to the catastrophic Italian situation in the winter of 1940-41 and disrupted all of Hitler's plans.

The British tried to take advantage of the situation, but Metaxas was too jealous of their international independence. In a friendly meeting in Athens, he received Field Marshal Sir Archibald Percival Wavell, future first viscount of Wavell, British representative and political-military chief for the Middle East and North Africa, but he only accepted some of the terms, as he literally said that: "*...his offers were stingy and insufficient, taking into account what Greece was risking...*" Nevertheless, he accepted the help of the British: Some troops were to help Greece inside its territory, the British would position others nearby and at the same time prepare for the possibility of a real and effective support by these troops in the future. Furthermore, this facilitated the creation of naval or aerial bases on Crete and another islands.

The progression of events resulted catastrophic for Mussolini, conflictive for Hitler and unsatisfactory for the British, who wanted to place an expeditionary army in Greece to stop the Axis Powers there. In the midst of this conflict of interests, Metaxas was superfluous, as he prejudiced all the interested parties, and hence, to facilitate matters, he conveniently died from a respiratory infection on the 29th January 1941. Never had a death been so well-timed, especially for the British, to whom the finger was always pointed accusing them of helping Metaxas to die. He was replaced by Alexandros Korizis, who held the gates of Greece wide open for Wavell's troops. Operation *«Marita»* was finally approved.

During the winter, the operations in the Balkans slowed down, but the Greeks continued to take the initiative. Mussolini counterattacked in March, suffering another defeat. On the 6th April, simultaneously with the operation in Yugoslavia, the Wehrmacht left from Bulgaria to invade Greece. Athens fell on the 27th April and by the 28th, the conquest was finished, lacking only a few trimmings.

OPERATIONS IN THE SOUTH OF YUGOSLAVIA AND GREECE.
SINCE 6TH TO 30TH APRIL, 1941
YUGOSLAVIA
BULGARIA
ALBANIA
TURKEY
3 G.A.
3 Armee
Pz. Gr. I
XI. AK
12. Armee
XXXXI. AK mot.
L. AK. (Res)
VII. Fl. K.
XVIII. Geb. K
XXX. AK
9th and 10th Italian Army
Danube river
Aegean Sea
Adriatic Sea
THRACE
MACEDONIA
THESSALY
PINDE
EUBEA
ATICA
PELOPONNESUS
CRETE
SAMOTHRACE
IMROS
LIMNOS
CORFU
Nis
Pleven
Botevgrad
SOFÍA
Jambol
Stara Zagora
Plovdiv
Kustendil
Prizren
Skutari
Skopje
Stip
Strumica
Petric
TIRANA
Elbasan
Prilep
Bitola
Xanthi
Komotini
Alexandrupolis
Serrai
Kabola
Edessa
Beve
Fiorina
Salónica
Raterine
Grebena
Serbja
Metsobon
Toannina
Larisa
Farsala
Balos
Domakos
Arta
Lamia
Topolia
Thermopylae
Molos
Atalante
Tanagra
Thebes
Chalkis
Erythral
Eleusis
Tatoi
ATHENS
Patras
Corinth
Megar
Argos
Nauplian
Tripolis
Kalamata
Malao
Maleme
Heraklion
Kasos
Metaxas Line
1st Aliakman Line
2nd Aliakman Line
Previous fortifications non built
Thermopylae´s fortifications
German attacks
Italian attacks
Allied evacuation
1 Central Macedonian Army and British expeditionary corps
2 Eastern Macedonian Army
3 Western Macedonian Army
4 Epirus´ Army
3 G.A. Yugoslavian Army
Airfields

The Commonwealth soldiers, who did not have enough time to embark at the ports of Peloponeso, surrendered to the German troops. (Bundesarchiv 101III-Mayr-014-06).

During the conquest of Greece, several historical-military events of certain interest took place. The deployment troops of Field Marshal Henry Maitland Wilson, the future first Baron of Wilson, which began on the 22nd February 1941, materialised in an effective manner, from the 4th March and consisted in a force of 57,660 men, 142 tanks of various models and tonnages, as well as an artillery force comprising more than 700 pieces. The majority of these British troops were New Zealanders and Australians, the minority originating from the mother country. By the end of March, they were completely deployed in Macedonia and Greece. From there, they became a nightmare for the Germans, as the Rumanian refineries at Ploesti (Rumania) were within the range of the British bombers, including those that were based on Crete itself. This island became the rearguard of the expeditionary army and various radar and radio equipment began to be installed there, as well as the construction of a naval base at Souda Bay.

Throughout this campaign, firstly in Yugoslavia and then in Greece, the flexibility and velocity of the German forces was demonstrated, as well as the testing of new tactics. Elements of the *Fallschirmregiment 2* (FJR2), transported on board one hundred and twenty Ju-52/3mg3e

Following page: In May 1941, the flag of the III Reich billowed at Acropolis. (Bundesarchiv 101I-164-0389-23a).

The new Dunkirk involved the embarkation of the British troops deployed in Greece and the loss of 14,500 men with all the heavy material, such as the Cruiser Mk.II tanks that appear in this snapshot. (Bundesarchiv 163-0318-14a).

As prelude to Operation *«Merkur»* and in order to cut off the British troops that were evacuating Greece via Peloponeso on the 26th April 1941, paratroopers from the FJR2 transported aboard DFS 230 gliders and triple-engine Junkers Ju 52/3mg took the bridge over the Corinth Canal in an audacious airborne attack. (Bundesarchiv 146-1977-122-166).

and six DFS 230 gliders, attacked the Corinth Canal on the 26th April, taking the bridge over the canal. The objective was to cut off the British forces and prevent their retreat. The paratroopers were unable to prevent the bridge from being blown up, but the rest of the operation was a success. On the 19th, it was decided to

The staff of the FJR2 directing the operations to take the bridge over the Corinth Canal. (Bundesarchiv 146-1977-122-15).

During the taking of the Corinth Canal, the German paratroopers suffered 63 dead, 16 missing and 174 wounded, another success with minimal losses. (Bundesarchiv 146-1977-163-05a y 4a).

evacuate the British troops if the Germans managed to cross the defensive line of Thermopylae, where they effectively arrived on the 20th. The evacuation of the men from the peninsular commenced on the 24th April, but during the final moments, many of them did not manage it. The last commander of the British troops, Major General Bernard Cyril Freyberg, the first Baron of Freyberg, left Greece almost at the same time as the surrender of Athens. General Wilson, commander of the expeditionary army, had done so on the 26th. General Freyberg headed for Crete, his new command post. His orders were to prevent Crete from being taken by the Axis Forces, at all costs.

The following day, Crete became the next target for the Axis. It marked the beginning of Operation *«Mercury»*. It was a challenge for the paratroopers and, as their commander General Kurt Student said: *"Crete was the grave of the German parachutists."*

After the destruction of the Corinth Canal bridge, the German sappers built another bridge to facilitate the passage between Continental Greece and Peloponnesus. (Bundesarchiv 146-2007-0108).

The Commonwealth troops left Greece, although a significant number of men didn't make it and were captured by the Germans. (IWM E2734).

But why Crete?

Crete (Kriti in Greek) is an island situated in the Aegean Sea. Its previous name, Candia was used until the beginning of the 20th Century. It is the largest of the Greek islands and the fifth largest in the Mediterranean Sea. Its surface is some 8,300 square kilometres and its coasts have a length of 1,040 km, along which are mostly found inaccessible steep cliffs, alternating with fine sand beaches. The average altitude is 200 metres, although it has some significant elevations, such as Mount Ida (2,460 metres) and Levka Ori (2,452 metres). All this results in a difficult orography, with small plains divided by mountains and valleys creating abrupt breaks in the landscape. Its rivers, or rather torrents in winter and drainage channels during the summer storms, are not very significant; only the River Mesara deserves to bear such a name. In such a tormented geography, it is easy to locate several bays and gulfs, like the Mirabello, and a multitude of capes, like Spatha.

Previus page: This photo, taken in 1943, shows the new bridge over the Corinth Canal built by the Germans. (Bundesarchiv 101I-178-1533-03a).

It has a Mediterranean climate, strongly influenced by the dominant winds, especially Westerlies and its sunny (south) and shady (north) slopes mean that the northern zone is always damper and more densely vegetated. However, deforestation caused by man, especially during the medieval wars as well as modern deforestation, has progressively increased its large-scale desertification and natural water deficiency. The following species stand out among the vegetation: Cypress, chestnut, salvia, thyme, oregano and finally, to a lesser degree, juniper, broom, oleander and myrtle.

During the Second World War, its population exceeded 300,000 inhabitants, although no reliable statistics exist. Nowadays, despite the exodus in the mid-20th Century, it exceeds 500,000 inhabitants.

Administratively, Crete is considered to be a region of Greece and it has four prefectures: One whose main city is the capital (Heraklion), Kania or Canea (previously Cha-

The Commonwealth troops were transported by ship to Crete, after leaving Greece. (IWM E2762).

nia), Rethymno and Lasithi. Its most important settlements are Chania (Khania), Rethymno, Ierepetra, Agios Nikolaos, Siteia, Moires, Neepoli, Tympaki and Kissamos.

Strategically, its geographical position has made it the centre of attention of the Eastern Mediterranean, as all the maritime routes Europe, Asia and North Africa are found within its sphere of influence. For this reason, it became vital during the 1940-1945 conflict. From its aerodromes, the bombers range of action was able to reach key points, including the Aegean Sea or Egypt and the fighters, though their range was cut in half, were also operative in almost a third of the East Mediterranean. Also from a naval point of view, although its ports were small, they were useful for re-provisioning. Souda Bay, next to Chania, is a very appropriate place for anchoring ships of a respectable size.

CHAPTER II
PREPARING THE GERMAN ATTACK ON CRETE

Airborne operations

Crete was the first and final large-scale airborne operation carried out by the German forces during the Second World War. The Germans had already conducted significant victories using this system at the Western Front, Norway, Belgium and Holland, though with reduced proportions in terms of space, time and the number of troops employed. Such an operation had only been studied on paper and in military manoeuvres. The first army to carry out paratrooper operations was the Soviet Army, which began studying them in 1930 and carrying out the first aerial landings during the 1935 and 1936 manoeuvres. In these, parachute jumps were made by personnel, as well as the launching of motorcycles and light vehicles.

In 1936, the Germans began testing on a large-scale what the Soviets had experimented with, immediately improving the doctrine and tactical options that were already known or supposed. A teaching and training centre was established at Stendal (60 km to the west of Berlin), developing new concepts, such as reserve parachutes. The students were trained during sixteen days in jumping, taking off after a jump, knowledge in the field of aviation, etc. The training immediately produced highly prepared soldiers for the formation of elite groups and special airborne units. By 1937, the *Luftwaffe* already had a paratrooper battalion. From the beginning, the triple-engine Junker Ju 52 was chosen as the aeroplane for transport and jumps. This machine could raise from twelve to fourteen very lightly equipped paratroopers: They only carried a pistol and six grenades, ammunition and three-days' food. In 1941, containers designed to transport rifles, machine guns and mortars were dropped together with the troops, which were then collected by the soldiers on the ground.

The doctrine of the paratrooper was surprise and it was supposed that the use of arms with greater fire power than those with which they were initially equipped would not be necessary. However, the first operations demonstrated the need for greater fire power, as surprise was not always the decisive weapon. The lessons learnt in Denmark and Norway, and later in Holland and at Eben Emael, contributed to the modification of the doctrine on the use of airborne forces, and when the moment arrived, these had grown in number and weaponry and above all, the doctrine of their use had been altered, following a recent and proven experience.

The operation en Belgium was a success: In less than 24 hours, the paratroopers aboard gliders, had taken two of the three bridges over the Albert Canal (the other one was blown up by the Belgians) and the paratroopers took the fort. In Holland, they were to capture and hold the aerodromes to the north of Rotterdam, until they were relieved, as a well as another three bridges that facilitated the passage of the land-based units that were to attack in that direction. This was also a strategic and tactical success, but it revealed the vulnerability of the team members, should they meet with resistance or be unable to successfully carry out the surprise. Several years later, Operation *«Market Garden»* proved, in almost the same scenario, that planning was extremely important in airborne operations and that the vulnerability of the troops conducting the operation was too high. This was something that Montgomery would certainly overlook, as he only saw the success and failed to detect the problems that would be caused there, which were then repeated on a large scale at Crete. Neither did he learn anything from it for his future actions at the end of the War.

Planning Operation *«Merkur»*.

Operation *«Merkur»* (the invasion of Crete) was assigned with significant forces: *XI Fliegerkorps* comprising the *7. Flieger-Division*, the *Luftlande Sturm Regiment* and the *5. Gebirgs-Division* (Mountain Division) as well as larger units. In the operation, 8,000 paratroopers were dropped over the island, being backed up by another 13,000 soldiers of the 5th Mountain Division, in addition to engineers, supporting light artillery, (both anti-tank and anti-aircraft) and various engineering material. A total of some 22,000 men were involved in the aerial conquest of Crete.

EThe main weapon was surprise, as it had been in previous attacks. However, the end

GERMAN BATTLE ORDER DURING *UNTERNEHMEN «MERCURY».*

LUFTWAFFE

Luftflotte 4
General Staff of the *Luftflotte 4*
Oberbefehlshaber: General der Flieger Alexander Löhr

VII *Fliegerkorps*
Kommandierender General (corps commander)
Generalfeldmarschall Wolfran "Roland" Freiherr von Richtofen
120 Dornier Do 17Z (Aerodrome of Tatoï), pertaining to the I./KG 2, II./KG 2 III./KG 2 y III./KG 3
40 Heinkel He 111H (Aerodrome of Eleusis), pertaining to the II./KG 76
80 Junkers Ju 88A-4 (Aerodrome of Eleusis), pertaining to the III./KG 30 y LG 1
150 Junkers Ju 87B *Stukas* (Aerodromes of Mycenae, Molaöi and Skarpanto), pertaining to the I./StG 2, III./StG 2 y I./StG 3
90 Messerschmitt Bf 110 (Aerodrome of Argos) pertaining to the ZG 76
90 Messerschmitt Bf 109 (Aerodrome of Molaöi) pertaining to the II./JG 77, III./JG 77 y I./LG 2

XI *Fliegerkorps*
Kommandierender General Generaloberst Kurt Arthur Benno Student
Aerial material: 502 Junkers Ju 52/3m g3e and between 70 y 80 model DFS 230 gliders pertaining to th I y II./*Kampfgeschwader z.b.V.* 1, *Kampfgruppe z.b.V.* 40, 60, 101, 102, 103, 105, 106, 172 y el I./*Luftlandegeschwader* 1.

Luftlande Sturmregiment 1 (Airborne Attack Regiment n.º 1)[1]
Generalmajor Eugen Meindl (Commander of *Gruppe West*)[1]
Stabkompanie[1]

Eugen Meindl, *Generalmajor der Fallschirmjägertruppen*, photographed in 1942; he is wearing the *Ritterkreuz*. (Bundesarchiv 183-2006-0124-503E2734).

First Lieutenant: *Oberstleutnant Von Seelen.*[1]
Stab Major: Major Franz Braun[1]
Officers: *Oberstleutnant* Schächter, Göttsche y Zierach[1]
Chief Medical Officer: *Oberstabsarzt* Dr. Heinrich Neumann[1]
Headquarters Office: *Hauptmann* Pettekau, *Oberfeldwebel* Gutheil, *Feldwebel* Erich y *Hauptfeldwebel* Koskialowski[1]

I./LLStR (First Battalion)[1]
Commander: *Major* Walter Koch (replaced by *Oberstabsarzt* Neumann)[1]
First Lieutenant: *Oberleutnant* Gerbershagen[1]
Chief of Staff: *Oberleutnant* Ofman[1]
Battalion Doctor: *Stabsartz* Dr. Jäger[1]
Kampfzugführer (senior non-commissioned officer): *Feldwebel* Urban[1]
Transmissions Unit: *Oberleutnant* Osius[1]
1.*kompanie*: *Oberleutnant* Alfred Genz[2]
2.kompanie: Hauptmann Gustav Altmann[2]
3.kompanie: Oberleutnant Wulf von Plessen[1]
4.kompanie: Oberleutnant Kurt Sarrazin[1]
Support weapons: Six heavy machine-guns, six heavy mortars[1]

II./LLStR (Second Battalion)[1]
Commander: *Major* Edgar Stentzler[1]
First Lieutenant: *Oberleutnant* Wolf[1]
Chief of Staff: *Oberleutnant* Stoltz[1]
Other officers of the General Staff: *Oberleutnant* Schelske, *Oberleutnant* Gobmann and *Leutnant* Braun[1]
Battalion Doctor: *Stabsartz* Dr. Rodpewig[1]
Kampfzugführer (Senior non-commissioned officer): *Hauptfeldwebel* Barabas[1]
5.kompanie: Oberleutnant Hesterich[1]
6.kompanie: Oberleutnant Pissin[1]
7.kompanie: Oberleutnant Barmetler[1]
8.kompanie: Oberleutnant Reinhardt[1]
Support Weapons: Six heavy machine guns, six 8 cm mortars and three 37 mm PaK cannons.[1]

III./LLStR (Third Battalion)[1]
Commander: *Major* Otto Scherber[1]
First Lieutenant: *Oberleutnant* Heinz[1]
Chief of Staff: *Oberleutnant* Horst Trebes[1]
Other officers in the General Staff: *Oberleutnant* Leib[1]
Battalion Doctor: *Stabsartz* Dr. Ellenbeck[1]
Kampfzugführer (Senior non-commissioned officer): *Oberfeldwebel* Ziehm[1]
9.kompanie: Oberleutnant Rudolf Witzig[1]
10.kompanie: Oberleutnant Schulte-Sasse[1]
11.kompanie: Oberleutnant Jung[1]
12.kompanie Oberleutnant Gansewig[1]
Support Weapons: Six heavy machine guns, six 8 cm mortars, four 37 mm PaK cannons, three 20 mm FlaK cannons.[1]

IV./LLStR (Fourth Battalion)[1]
Commander: *Hauptmann* Walter Gericke[1]
First Lieutenant: *Oberleutnant* Hengelhardt[1]
Battalion Doctor: *Stabsartz* Dr. Diehm[1]
N-zugführer: Oberfeldwebel Daniels[1]
13.kompanie: Oberleutnant Sauer[1]
14.kompanie: Hauptmann Kiessel[1]
15.kompanie: Oberleutnant Dobke[1]
16.kompanie: Oberleutnant Hoefeld (sapper paratroopers)[1]
Support Weapons: Six heavy machine guns, six 8 cm mortars, four 37 mm PaK, two 20 mm FlaK, 1 medical unit[1]

The participation of the air force (not only used for dropping the paratroopers, transporting and supplying the troops), was vital for carrying out Operation Merkur. Units from the German *VIII. Fliegerkorps* and the *Italian Comando Aeronautica Egeo* were employed. The illustrations in these pages show some of the models used in the conquest of Crete. From top to bottom:

- Junkers Ju 87R-2 *Stuka* was flown by *major* Walter Sigel. *Kommandeur* of I./St.G 3, stationed at Micenas.
- Fiat CR.42 *Falco* from the 162 *Squadriglia CT.*
- Messerschmitt Bf 109E-7 from the *Stab* III./*Jagdgeswader* 77, stationed at Molai.
- Messerschmitt Bf 110E-1 from the II./*Zerstörergeswader* 76, stationed at Argos.
- Junkers Ju 88A-4 from the III./LG 1 stationed at Elesius.
- Dornier Do 17Z from the I.*Kampfgeswader* 2 *«Holzhammer»*, based at Tatoi.
- Dornier Do 17 Z from the 1./*Kampfgeswader* 3, based at Tatoi.
- Heinkel He 111 H from the II.*Kampfgeswader* 26, based at Eleusis.
- CANT Z.1007 bis *Airone* from the *210.ª Squadriglia BT (50 Gruppo BT).*

Artwork: Luis Fresno Crespo and Julio López Caeiro.
The illustrations are not reproduced to the same scale.

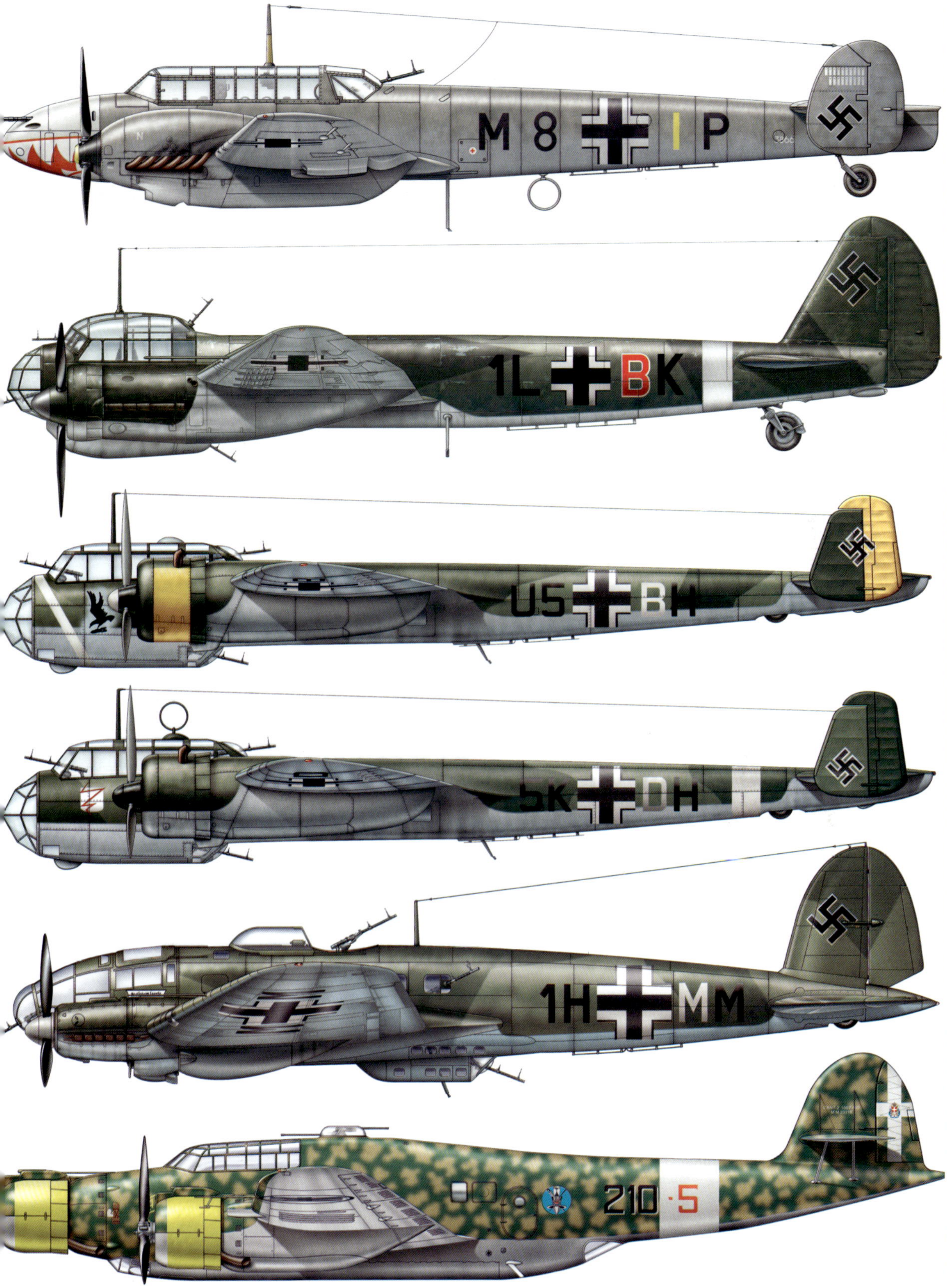
M8 IP
1L BK
U5 BH
5K DH
1H MM
210 -5

FRESNO'S

Junkers Ju 87R-2 *Stuka* from the *II.Gruppestab./St.G 77*, based at Mycenae, used against the Royal Navy ships in May 1941.

Artwork: Luis Fresno Crespo.

Kampftruppe Mürbe
Kompanie: *Leutnant* Mürbe (72 *Fallschirmjäger*, three 37 mm PaK.)
Stabkompanie: *Major* Fran Braun (90 *Fallschirmjäger* and three 3 detachments of gliders)
Fernmeldekompanie: Oberleutnant Osius (130 *Fallschirmjäger*)

7.Flieger-Division (7th Airborne Division)
Generalleutnant Willhelm Süssman[2]
Fallsch. Pionier-Bataillon 7[2]
Commander: *Major* Liebach[2]
1.kompanie: *Oberleutnant* Adolff[2]
2.kompanie: *Oberleutnant* Tietjen[2]
3.*kompania: Leutnant* Häffner[6]
Fallsch. Artillerie-Abteilung 7[6]
Commander: *Major* Böde[6]
Fallsch. MG-Bataillon 7 (Machine Gun Battalion)[6]
Commander: *Hauptmann* Schulz[6]
Fallsch. Panzerjäger-Abteilung 7 (Anti-tank Battalion)[6]
Commander: *Hauptmann* Schmitz[6]
Fs-Flak-MG-Bataillon 7[6]
Commander: *Hauptmann* Baier[6]
Fallsch. Sanitäts Abteilung 7
Commander: *Oberstarbzt*, Dr. Berg
1/*Fs Sanitäts Abteilung* 7: Dr. Mallison[2]
2/*Fs Sanitäts Abteilung* 7: Dr. Langemayer[4]
3/*Fs Sanitäts Abteilung* 7: Dr Siebert[1]
4/*Fs Sanitäts Abteilung* 7: Dr. Steidel (Hospital at Maleme)
Fallschirmjäger Regiment 1[4]
Commander: *Oberst* Bruno Bräuer (Commander of *Gruppe Mitte*)[4]
Stabskompanie: *Major* Count von Úxkull[4]
I/FJR1[4]
Commander: *Major* Walther[4]
1.*kompanie*: *Oberleutnant* Götte[4]
2.*kompanie*: *Hauptmann* Gröschke[4]
3.*kompanie*: *Oberleutnant* Von Brandis[4]
4.*kompanie*: *Leutnant* Kiebitz[5]
II/FJR1[4]
Commander: *Hauptmann* Burckhardt[4]
5.*kompanie*: *Oberleutnant* Hermann[4]
6.*kompanie*: *Hauptmann* Dunz[4]
7.*kompanie*: [4]
8.*kompanie*: *Oberleutnant* Platow[4]
III/FJR1[4]
Commander: *Major* Shulz[4]
9.*kompanie*: *Oberleutnant* Singer[4]
10.*kompanie*: *Oberleutnant* Egger[4]
11.*kompanie*: *Oberleutnant* Becker[4]
12.*kompanie*: *Oberleutnant* Vossahge[5]
Fallschirmjäger Regiment 2[3]
Commander: *Oberst* Alfred Sturm[3]
Stabskompanie[3]
I/FJR2[3]
Commander: *Major* Kroh[3]
1.*kompanie*: *Oberleutnant* Schindler[3]

2.*kompanie*: *Oberleutnant* Jahnke[3]
3.*kompanie*: *Oberleutnant* von Roon[3]
4.*kompanie*: *Hauptmann* Marawetz
II/FJR2[4]
Commander: *Hauptmann* Schirmer[4]
5.*kompanie*: *Oberleutnant* Thiel[4]
6.*kompanie*: *Oberleutnant* Nagele[4]
7.*kompanie*: *Oberleutnant* Zimmermann[4]
8.*kompanie*: *Oberleutnant* Paul[4]
III/FJR2[3]
Commander: *Hauptmann* Wiedemann[3]
9.*kompanie*: *Oberleutnant* Begeman[3]
10.*kompanie*: *Oberleutnant* Semder[3]
11.*kompanie*: *Oberleutnant* Pabst[3]
12.*kompanie*: *Oberleutnant* Hinz[3]
13.*kompanie* (*Infanteriegeschütz*): *Oberleutnant* Platz[3]
14.*kompanie* (*Panzerjäger*): *Oberleutnant* Hatze[3]

Fallschirmjäger Regiment 3[2]
Commander: *Oberst* Richard Heidrich[2]
Stabskompanie: *Oberleutnant* Heckel[2]
I/FJR 3[2]
Commander: *Hauptmann* von der Heydte[2]
1.*kompanie*: *Oberleutnant* Hädrich[2]
2.*kompanie*: *Oberleutnant* Knoche[2]
3.*kompanie*: *Oberleutnant* Straeller-Pohl[2]
4.*kompanie*: *Oberleutnant* Peiser[2]
II/FJR 3[2]
Commander: *Major* Derpa[2]
5.*kompanie*: *Oberleutnant* Staab[2]
6.*kompanie*: *Oberleutnant* Stangemberg[2]
7.*kompanie*: *Oberleutnant* Neuhoff[2]
8.*kompanie*: *Oberleutnant* Böhmler[2]
III/FJR 3[2]
Commander: *Major* Heilmann[2]
9.*kompanie*: *Oberleutnant* Heymann[2]
10.*kompanie*: *Oberleutnant* Pagels[2]
11.*kompanie*: *Oberleutnant* Kerstens[2]
12.*kompanie*: *Oberleutnant* Vollquardsen[2]
13.*kompanie* (*Infanteriegeschütz*): *Oberleutnant* Schimkatt[2]
14.*kompanie* (*Panzerjäger*): *Oberleutnant* Günther[2]

5. Gebirgs-Division
Commander: *Generalmajor* Julius Ringel
Gerbirgs-Artillerie-Regiment 95
Commander: *Oberstleutnant* Wittmann
I./95 *Abteilung*: *Major* Von Sternbach
II./95 *Abteilung*: *Major* Raithel
Gebirgs-Pionier-Bataillon 95:
Commander: *Major* Schaette
Panzerjäger-Abteilung 95:
Commander: *Major* Bindermann
Aufsklärungsabtteilung 95
Commander: *Major* Graf Castell zu Castell
Narischabtteilung 95
Commander: *Major* Nolte
Gebirgsjäger-Regiment 85

Commander: *Oberst* August Krakau
I *Abteilung: Major* Treck
II *Abteilung: Major* Esch
III *Abteilung: Major* Fett
Gebirgsjäger-Regiment 100
Commander: *Oberst* Willibald Utz
I *Abteilung: Major* Schrank
II *Abteilung: Major* Friedmann
III *Abteilung: Major* Ehall
Gebirgsjäger-Regiment 141[7]
Commander: *Obest* Maximilian Jais

Kradschtz Abteilung 55 (landed on the 23rd of May)
FlaK-Abteilung 73 (landed on the 25th of May)
FlaK-Abteilung (mot.) 609 (landed on the 24th of May)
Panzer Regiment 31 de la *5. Panzer-Division* (landed on the 27th of May)

---

1 First wave *Gruppe West* (target Maleme)
2 First wave *Gruppe Mitte* (targets Chania and Souda)
3 Second wave *Gruppe Mitte* (target Rethymno)
4 Second wave *Gruppe Ost* (target Heraklion)
5 Reserve units
6 Units transported by sea
7. The *Gebirgsjäger-Regiment 141* was part of the *6. Gebirgs-Division*. It was temporarily adjoined to the *5. Gebirgs-Division* for Operation *Merkur»*

result was different to that expected. Doctrine specified that the paratroopers should take their targets by surprise (either jumping or lan-

Gebirgsjäger waiting for the order to board the Junkers Ju 52 that would take them to Crete. (Bundesarchiv 146-1981-159-24).

ding directly on them, or taking nearby zones and attacking immediately) until they were quickly relieved by stronger units to then operate as forces acting at the forefront of the actions of more classical and stronger units. The paratroopers also served as observers and took highways and road junctions, as well as other objectives immediately ahead of the rest of the forces. However, several obstacles were to negatively affect the parachute action. In the first place, and Crete being an island, a substantial domination of the sea was necessary, which did not take place. The British Navy was infinitely superior to the Italian Navy, the only one it was confronted with, and it was well supported by smaller German and captured Greek ships (only for transportation). Originally, the OKW had considered an amphibious operation, but this was set aside, as the sea was dominated by the powerful Royal Navy.

Generaloberst Kurt Student personally prepared an aerial attack project that he presented to Hitler in a meeting in which he was accompanied by Göring. It was held on the 21st April 1941. The *Führer* finally accepted and signed on the 25th; it was *Führer* Order Number 28. The premise of this Order was that the *Luftwaffe* should neutralise British Navy, destroying it, while the island's defences would be "*previously softened*" with bombardment operations.

The strategic objective of this order was the conquest of the island in order to convert it into an operations base from which the *Luftwaffe* could control the movements of the British in the Eastern Mediterranean. The order specified that its execution should commence on the 15th May. Just three weeks were granted for the preparation and execution of the order. However, the order was impossible to follow, as the troops designated to carry it out were disseminated throughout Europe and they had to be transferred to Greece. The last of the paratrooper contingents arrived on the 14th May, just 24 hours prior to the date initially established for the mission's completion. Furthermore, the Ju 52/3mg3e assigned were not available, as they had just been used exhaustively in the conquest of Greece. At the initial moment of the resource gathering process, they were found under compulsory inspection periods, which seriously compromised (if not fulfilled), their very safety and that of those they were transporting. As many as 502 of the aeroplanes assigned to the taking of Crete were in this situation.

Other logistical problems harassed the German command: The troops' food supply was not secure, as the landing of the British Expeditionary body, its later embarkation and the Balkans invasion troops had finished off the food reserves in Greece and also with those transported by the invasion army. Another also very important "food" was also being delayed: aircraft fuel, which was transported from Italy in three tankers that were unable to reach its destination. The Corinth Canal was their only possible route, open to British attack, but it was closed due to the collapse of a bridge (blown up by the British), during the recent paratrooper attack. The canal remained unused due to the aforementioned collapse, until the German divers managed to partially clean it and tankers were able to go through. The fuel was transported in drums to the makeshift airfields from which the 502 aeroplanes would take off and this greatly delayed the refilling of the reserves, as it had to be carried out manually, with significant effort. All these problems: The concentration of personnel, the requisitioning of ships and the accumulation of fuel delayed the start of the operation by five days.

A new problem was added to those previously mentioned: The German Intelligence and its confidence in certain premises. In the first place, no updated photos were distributed among the pilots until the 19th, just 24 hours beforehand, and these had not been interpreted adequately. The intelligence was based on information from Greek and Italian sources, which estimated the defences as two brigades of infantry, plus an undetermined number of personnel evacuated from Greece after its occupation by Germany. Intelligence assumed that these troops were demoralised, poorly armed and badly commanded, and that no special defences had been built around the existing airports. They had not detected the wildness of the terrain, which would greatly hinder both landing and posterior movements. Neither had they detected the camouflaged positions that were defending Maleme, Souda Bay,

Previus page: The requisition of ships for transporting troops was another reason why the start of the invasion of Crete was delayed. In the photograph, taken on the 29th May 1941, a group of *Gebirgsjäger* are making themselves comfortable in a Greek fishing boat that would take them to Crete. (Bundesarchiv 146-1981-033-36a).

Rethymno and Heraklion. They were also mistaken about the attitude of the civilian population, who according to the Intelligence information, were inclined towards the departure of the British and they thought that they would receive the German forces in a friendly manner; information that was highly contradictory with reality, as will be seen later on.

Nevertheless, the attack forces hurriedly conducted some tests in Greece itself. On the airfields that would later be used for the departure, take-offs, landings and attacks were practiced. The pilots and paratroopers soon identified their main enemy, the dust. Southern Greece, like Crete, is very arid and the aeroplane manoeuvres caused enormous dust clouds which impeded vision over a considerable distance and period of time of twenty to thirty minutes. It was decided to dampen the terrain of the aerodromes before commencing the operations, but though this option could be taken there in Greece, it was clearly not going to be possible on Crete. The dust resulted in delays in the training and then during the operation, as the stream of aeroplanes came and went from the island. These delays had a noticeable effect on the progress of the action. The German High Command decided to complement the aerial attack with an amphibious landing. The mountaineers of the *5. Gebirgs-Division,* commanded by *Generalmajor* Julius Ringel were chosen for the task and transport was sought among the available civilian ships. Only one petition for aerial support was dispatched, for the *Luftwaffe* to defend these ships from the air from a possible attack by the greatly superior Royal Navy. The fleets, made up of patrol boats, fishing boats, caiques, etc., had to transport all the material required by the mountaineers: Cannons, mortars, wheeled tanks and other vehicles. These were very heterogeneous and certainly not the most appropriate for the intended purpose. The pressing time and lack of sea domination, as well as the inexistence of their own naval resources, ended up reducing them to a mere group that provided support to the airborne units only during the final moments of the invasion.

Definitively, and although it may seem not very German, the great problem was the improvisation and lack of information on the objectives to be taken, which undoubtedly led to the results are all familiar with.

CHAPTER III
THE CONFRONTING FORCES

Finally, the German Command decided to rely almost solely on the aerial superiority of the *Luftwaffe*. Its objective established definitively twenty-four hours before the start was the capture of the island's three main aviation fields. Prior to this, three different attack plans had been considered: The first, very ambitious, planned an attack on the seven main points of the island, which would have to be taken simultaneously by paratroopers and mountaineers. This plan was too ambitious and left many flanks open, for which reason Göring rejected the plan. The second option was to take the Maleme aviation field, for the immediate take-off of the troops in Chania and Souda Bay. Once this zone was taken, the easternmost part of the island, an attack would be launched fanning out on towards the rest. Its advantage was securing a rearguard and solid provisioning point, but it was predictable that the advance on the rest of the island would be very difficult, as the defenders would be able to attack the flanks from the coast during the advance. Furthermore, it was predicted that continuous attacks would be made from the mountains and inland mountain passes, in addition to leaving the aerodromes in the hands of the Allies. A third possibility, which was the one finally adopted, consisted in a two-wave attack on four targets: Maleme and Chania (Souda Bay) in the morning and Rethymno and Heraklion in the afternoon, continuing with the arrival of more troops that would complete the action. Finally, it was decided to carry out an intensive bombardment beforehand, with the Dornier Do 17 and Junkers Ju 88 bombers, from two aerial take-off positions, while the Messerschmitt Bf 109 and Me 110 simultaneously machine-gunned the neighbouring areas and roads. The action began with a first wave attacking the aerodrome of Maleme, Chania and Souda

Bay, by the *Luftlande-Sturmregiment* (LLStR) and the *Fallschirmjäger-Regiment* 3 (FJR3). Eight hours later, a second wave with the *Fallschirmjäger-Regiment* 1 and 2 (FJR1 and FJR2) attacked the aerodromes of Rethymno and Heraklion. The objectives should be fulfilled within the first twenty-four hours. Then, once the aerodromes had been secured, the reinforcements would begin to arrive by air. Next, the conquered terrain would be increased, with Souda Bay and the small ports along the north coast, followed by the conquest of the rest of the island, which was to be carried out by the mountaineers, supported by the marine infantry and the paratroopers. Nobody predicted the complications that arose later.

The German forces designated for the attack

It was decided in the *Führer's* headquarters that *Generaloberst* Alexander Löhr would lead command the whole operation, in the function of commander of the IV *Luftflotte*. The Air Force: Transport, fighter and attack aeroplanes from the VIII *Fliegerkorps* would be commanded by *Generalfeldmarschall* Wolfran "Roland" Freiherr von Richthofen and the airborne forces, the XI *Fliegerkorps* compri-

Generaloberst Alexander Löhr, *General der Flieger*, was designated to lead the entire operation, being commander of the IV *Luftflotte* as he was. (Bundesarchiv 146-1969-041-30).

sing the 7. *Flieger-Division* as well as the 5. *Gebirg-Division* would be under the command of *Generaloberst* Kurt Student.

The VIII *Fliegerkorps* was equipped with 570 fighter, attack and bomber planes (see box on page 20). The XI *Fliegerkorps*, commanded by *Generalmajor* Eugen Meindl, disposed of a fleet of transport aeroplanes totalling 502 Junkers Ju 52/3mg3e and 70 (other sources cite this figure as 80) DFS 230 gliders. The 7. *Flieger-Division*, commanded by *Generalmajor* Süssmann, had some 11,000 men, of whom 8,060 were to take part in the initial attack. The 5. *Gebirgs-Division* had 13,980 men, who were to be transported by aeroplane and in the naval fleets, making the final total of 29,040 men comprising the German forces, with marine infantry troops, marines and other technicians supporting the various actions.

LThe two fleets (in three different forces) were comprised, as already mentioned, of requisitioned Greek ships, a destroyer, some

Generalmajor Julius Ringel, *General der Gebirgstruppen*, commander of the 5. *Gebirgs-Division*. He was awarded the *Ritterkreuz* on the 28th June 1941. (Bundesarchiv 183-R63746).

British troops landing at Alexandria destined for Crete, on the 14th of November 1940. (IWM E1143).

Italian torpedo launchers and submarines. All this was under the command of *Konteradmiral* Schüster, perhaps the most pessimistic of the commanders, as the heterogeneity and poor safety of his ships was added to the possible actions of the British Navy..

Defence preparations

The British had been occupying the island for six months when the attack began. Although they had arrived there to transform it

The commander in chief for the Middle East, General Sir Archibald Wavell, landed in Souda Bay on the 13th of November 1940, in order to inspect the garrison in Crete. (IWM E1179).

Brigadier General Tidbury, first commander of the CREO-FORCE, examining Souda Bay, in order to evaluate the possible measures to take to improve the defence of the island. (IWM E1169).

into an observation and logistical support point, the development of the war in the Balkans had led them to become the main defensive force of the island. The progressive settlement of the British detachments and the tacit recognition of the same facilitated the creation of plans that would later be useful in the event of an Italian-German attack. Since November 1940, when the first British arrived, the commander of the British troops in the Middle East and North Africa, General Sir Archibald Wavell, had structured a plan of action in the Eastern Mediterranean. In this, Crete was only considered as a secondary objective, but Wavell's idea was that this was no reason to disregard its defence. Nevertheless, and despite the priority that the British Prime Minister, Sir Winston Churchill, had given the island in October 1940, Wavell always kept it in the background of his objectives, as demonstrated by the fact that it had had seven different commanders in just six months. However, the first commander in chief of the British forces, Brigadier O. H.

Tidbury, had already established some defensive premises. These consisted in it being important to maintain Souda Bay and Maleme and as both settlements were semi-isolated from the rest, it was fundamental that they dispose of independent self-defences and above all that they be self-sufficient.

Tidbury's report predicted airborne attacks on Maleme, Rethymno and Heraklion and a possible amphibious landing close to the latter two places, developing a plan that fitted like a glove to what the Germans would later do. However, the economical and logistical, and above all personnel difficulties prevented Tidbury's defensive plan from being carried out and the plan remained on paper waiting for another more appropriate moment. Nevertheless, both Tidbury and his successors applied for at least the necessary administrative preparations to be carried out, which was not feasible either. The different commanders in chief of the island became familiar with the situation and were relieved without taking any measures at all.

Already during the first moments of the invasion of Greece, the then commander of the island, Major General E. C. Weston of the Royal Navy, asked for two brigades of infantry to be sent to the island, as well as artillery, engineers and aeroplanes, but his request was refused. He also insisted in the improvement of the roads (for want of a better word), which constituted the route infrastructure, but neither the Greek authorities nor the British military answered him. In his last report, Weston assured that under those conditions, the island would be a grave faced with the more than likely German attack.

However, the creation of defensive infrastructure was carried out at Souda Bay, as the Royal Navy began to use it as a provisioning point and decided to establish a defensive system at the port to improve security. Firstly, they dug trenches around the points to be defended, as well as in the nearby hills and then a few anti-aircraft cannons were installed.

The reality was that when they finally had to leave Greece precipitately, many of the weapons that would later be necessary for the defence of the island were abandoned there. Invaluable time had been lost. In May 1941, when it was clear that Crete was the next target, was when the organised defence of the island really began, but those six months that had passed were irretrievable.

ABofors cannon originating from Egypt, being unloaded at Souda Bay in November. (IWM E1160).

The Greek-British deployment before the invasion

Wavell's bloody-mindedness, advocating that the next step in the Axis advance after

Two more shots of the landing of the troops, weapons, provisions and vehicles originating from Egypt and destined to form part of the garrison on Crete, in November 1940. (IWM E1161 y E1166).

A column of British Bren carriers, recently landed in Souda Bay, being cheered by the residents of Chania (above) and then being blessed by the local Bishop, surrounded by the residents (below). (IWM E1207 y E1199).

Artwork: Julio López Caeiro.

General Wavell inspecting a 3.7 inch anti-aircraft position on Crete. (IWM E1188).

Greece would be Cyprus or Syria, maintained the island deprived of preventative actions for its defence. Just six weeks before what was to be the definitive start date of the attack, and very begrudgingly, Wavell began to supply the men and equipment that had previously been applied for. In fact, he didn't take very much interest in it, as his idea was that the bulk of the defenders should be extracted from continental Greece. Nevertheless, he began to send the material, ammunition, spares, etc..., that the defence required.

The last British commander in Greece, General Bernard Cyril Freyberg, commander of the New Zealand troops, was charged with commanding the defence of Crete. He took charge of this no sooner than he had set foot on the island after abandoning the peninsular and he didn't like what he found. None of the aviation fields had adequate characteristics. In fact, only one of them had an asphalt runway. The aerial units for the defence were minimal and the anti-aircraft capacity of the aerodromes was practically non-existent, the reason for which the risk was not taken to send many aircraft and certainly, with the idea of removing them as soon as the German attack began, as occurred on the 19th May. Not even the most basic defensive works had been carried out, such as trenches or the installation of mine fields and barbed wire.

The scarcity of sapper material was such that the lids of metallic containers had to be used as spades to construct the defences and they improvised with cloths and fishing nets to camouflage the pieces of artillery. This was almost non-existent and the pieces received were used to defend the coast, aerodromes and communication routes, especially the bridges. The artillery consisted in obsolete pieces of Italian and French artillery of many different calibres. The collective and individual equipment of the fighters was very tight and scarce. In fact, the Greek fighters had just one rifle per two men. They did have some tanks however, and in addition to these, 16 light and medium tanks were sent by way of reinforcements, as well as another six infantry ones, which arrived on the 15th May, the day initially planned for the German attack. Freyberg had a difficult mission that he did not manage to fulfil and that would later raise doubts about his capacity for command and decision.

The Allied battle order

Freyberg was certain that the main German effort would be developed in an aerial landing, accompanied by another amphibious one, and so he decided to cover the most useful beaches for a landing on the northern part of the island, Canea and Souda Bay, as well as three aerodromes. This meant dividing the forces, but it secured a more efficient defence of the strategic points. Against this distribution, weighed the fact that once the action had been started, the land communications, which were already difficult enough, would become impossible. With respect to the transmission of orders, this would also be complicated, as the telephone lines and radio could become unusable and hence the commands of each independent group would have to make decisions itself, a difficult matter within the very strict British command system, as we will see later on.

Freyberg positioned his forces according to the following distribution:

- In the Heraklion sector, he placed the 14th Infantry Brigade, an Australian battalion and two Greek regiments, with artillery and 11 tanks of various models.
- In the Rethymno sector, he deployed five Australian battalions, two Greek ones and various logistical units, with artillery and 14 tanks.
- Defending Souda Bay, very heterogeneous units were positioned: Rangers, hussars, an Australian brigade and a Greek battalion, with artillery and adjunct units.
- At Maleme and its zone of influence, he placed the two New Zealand brigades, two Greek battalions, artillery, twelve tanks of different types and the corresponding logistic units.
- The Royal Air Force took up positions at Maleme and Heraklion: 12 Bristol *Blenheim,* 8 Hawker *Hurricanes* and 18 Gloster *Gladiators*. All the machines that had survived the previous attacks on the 20th May took off for Egypt, just before the paratrooper attack.
- In turn, the Royal Navy disposed of four independent naval forces including several cruisers and destroyers. These were to be supported by another four fleets of destroyers and torpedo launchers to prevent an amphibious attack and to collaborate with the anti-aircraft defence. The other mission of the naval forces would be the

Although the number of tanks in the garrison at Crete was very scarce (some 37 models), they were a menace to the airborne German troops, who were initially devoid of heavy weaponry. The illustration shows a Mk. VIB light tank.

Artwork: Julio López Caeiro.

Allied Battle Order

Headquarters (HQ) CREOFORCE. (Situated to the east of Chania).
Major General Bernard Cyril Freyberg.
- Fonce Headquarters Signals.
- Commander Royal Artillery.
- Cheif Engineer.
- Assistant Director of Supplies and Transport.
- Assistant Director of Ordnance Services.
- Assistant Director of Medical Services.
- 42nd Field Company, Royal Engineers.
- Royal Engineers Stores Depot.
- 1003rd Docks Operation Company.

Reserve Forces.
- Squadron C, 3rd The King's Own Hussars. (6 Vicker Mk. VI)
- Squadron B, 7th Royal Tank Regiment. (5 Matilda Mk. II)
- 1st Battalion, Welsh Regiment.

Heraklion Sector
Brigadier General Brian Herbert Chappel.
General Staff Troops:
- Section of the 1007th Docks Operation Company.
- Section of the 1038th Arab Stevedore Company.

14th Infantry Brigade:
- General Staff of the 14th Infantry Brigade.
- 14th Infantry Brigade Signal Section.

Infantry:
- 2nd Battalion Black Watch. Major A. A. Pitcairn. Temporarily replaced by A. K. Hamilton.
- 2nd Battalion York & Lancaster Regiment. Lieutenant Colonel A. Gilroy.
- 1st Argyll and Sutherland Highlanders. Lieutenant Colonel R. C. B. Anderson. (situa ted in the Tymbaky Sector).

Adjoined units:
- 2nd Battalion, the Leicestershire Regiment. Lieutenant Colonel Cox.
- 2nd/4th Australian Infantry Battalion.
- 7th Medium Regiment Royal Artillery (lacked artillery and operated as infantry).
- 3rd Regiment of Greek Infantry.
- 7th Regiment of Greek Infantry.
- Greek Garrison Battalion (ex 5th "Crete" Greek Division).

Engineers:
- Commander Royal Engineers.
- Una sección de la 42nd Fiel Company, Royal Engineers.

Artillery:
- 234th Medium Battery Royal Artillery (13 pieces of 75-100 mm).
- Elements of the 7th Australian Light AA Battery (six 40 mm Bofors cannons).
- A section of the 156th Light AA Battery (two 40 mm Bofors cannons).
- A section of the 15th Coast Artillery Regiment (two 4 inch pieces).
- A section of the C Battery, Heavy Anti-Aircraft Battery (four 3 inch pieces).
- A section of the 23rd Light AA Battery, Royal Marines (four 3 inch pieces).

Royal Armoured Corps:
Six tanks Cruiser Mk II of the 6th Hussars
Five light tanks Vickers Mk VI from Squadron B of the 7th RTR (three tanks deployed at Timbaki).
Services:
- 189th Company Field Ambulance.
- Royal Army Medical Corps.
- Royal Army Service Corps.
- Royal Ordnance Corps.

Rethymno Sector
Brigadier George Alan Vasey.
General Staff Troops:
- Signal Construction Section.
- Australian Signal Section.

19th Australian Brigade
- General Staff of the 19th Australian Brigade. Lieutenant Colonel I. R. Campbell Military Commander of Rethymno.

Infantry:
- 2nd/1st Australian Infantry Battalion. Lt. Col. Ian R. Campbell.
- 2nd/7th Australian Infantry Battalion. Lt. Col Theo Walker.
- 2nd/8th Australian Infantry Battalion.
- 2nd/11th Australian Infantry Battalion. Major Ray Sandover.
- 2nd/1st Australian Machine Gun Company.

Adjoined units:
- 4th Regiment of Greek Infantry.
- 5th Regiment of Greek Infantry.
- Two battalions of local Greek militia.
- Cretan police.

Engineers:
- 2nd/8th Field Regiment, Royal Australian Engineers.

Artillery:
- A section of the 106th Royal Horse Artillery (two 2 pound anti-tank pieces).
- X Coast Defence Artillery, Royal Australian Artillery (two 4 inch pieces).
- 2nd/3rd Field Regiment, Royal Australian Artillery (fourteen 75 mm and 100 mm piece).

Royal Armoured Corps:
- Fourteen Vickers Mk VI tanks (in various states of preservation) from the 7th RTR.

Services:
- Australian Army Service Corps Detachments.
- Deputy Assistant Director of Ordnance Services, Rethymno Sector.
- 2nd/1st Australian Ordnance Store Company and miscellaneous Detachments.

Souda Bay Sector:
Major General de la Marina Real E. C. Weston.
General Staff Troops:
- General Staff of MNBDO (Mobile Naval Base Defence Organization)
- Headquarters (HQ) of the Mobile Reserve.
- Commander of the Mobile Reserve: Major General Eric Culpeper Weston.
- Souda Sector Signals (Army).

Infantry:
- 9th Battalion, King's Royal Rifle Corps. (The Ranger).
- Northumberland Hussars.
- 102nd Anti-Aircraft Regiment Royal Horse Artillery, used as infantry.
- 106th Royal Horse Artillery, used as infantry.
- 16th Australian Infantry Brigade Composite Battalion.
- 17th Australian Infantry Brigade Composite Battalion.
- 1st Royal Perivolian Composite Battalion.
- 2nd/2nd Field Regiment, Royal Australian Artillery, used as infantry
- 2nd Regiment of Greek Infantry
- Group A Royal Australian Artillery personal.
- Group B Royal Australian Engineers personal.

Engineers:

- Commander Royal Engineers.
- 42nd Field Company, Royal Engineers (less one section).
- Crete Composite Company, Royal Engineers.
- Australian Engineers and Australian Army Service Corps Stevedores.
- New-Zealand Stevedores.

Artillery:

Group M:

- General Staff 52nd Light AA Regiment, Royal Artillery.
- 151st Heavy AA Battery, Royal Artillery (eight 3.7 inch pieces).
- 129th Light AA Battery, Royal Artillery (twelve 40 mm Bofors pieces).
- 156th Light AA Battery, Royal Artillery (elements) (two 40 mm Bofors pieces).
- 7th Australian Light AA Battery (a section of two 40 mm Bofors pieces).
- 23rd Light AA Battery, Royal Marines (two sections of machine guns).

Group S:

- General Staff 2nd Heavy AA Regiment. Royal Marines.
- A Heavy AA Battery, Royal Marines (eight 3 inch pieces).
- 234th Heavy AA Battery, Royal Artillery (eight 3.7 inch pieces).
- 304th Battery Search Lights, Royal Artillery (20 search lights).
- 106th Royal Horse Artillery (a section of two 2 pound pieces).
- 15th Coast Regiment (less a section), Royal Artillery (four 6 inch pieces, two 4 inch pieces, two 12 pound pieces and two search lights)
- Z Coast Defence Battery, Royal Marines.
- 207th Coast Defence Battery.
- Batteries B and Y of the Nottinghamshire Yeomanry.

Mobile Naval Defence Units:

- Mobile Naval Base Defence Force Organization Landing and Maintenance Unit.
- Mobile Naval Base Defence Force Organization Pioneer and Labour Group.

Services:

- 231st Mechanical Transport Company.
- 101st Petrol Company.
- 37th Detail Issue Depot.
- Detachments from the 1st and 26th Field Bakeries (field bread factories).
- 5th Indian Brigade Workshops.
- 2nd Heavy Anti-Aircraft Workshops, Royal Marines.
- 52nd Light Anti-Aircraft Workshops.
- Ordnance Officer Docks.
- Deputy Assistant Director of Ordnance Services.
- Ordnance Depot.
- Ammunition Depot.
- 1st Tented Hospital, Royal Navy.
- 189th Field Ambulance, Royal Army Medical Corps (less a company).
- 4th Light Field Ambulance, Royal Army Medical Corps.
- Detachments from the 2/1st, 2/2nd and 2/7th Australian Field Ambulance.
- 2nd Armoured Division Hygiene Section.
- 48th Field Hygiene Section.

Six companies of workers:

- 605th Palestine Pioneer Company.
- 1004th Cypriot Pioneer Company.
- 1005th Cypriot Pioneer Company.
- 1006th Cypriot Pioneer Company.
- 1007th Cypriot Pioneer Company.
- 1008th Cypriot Pioneer Company.

Maleme and Chania Sector
Brigadier General Edward Puttick.
General Staff Troops:

- General Staff of the New Zealand Division.
- Cuartel General (HQ) 2nd New Zealand.
- New Zealand Headquarters Signals.
- Squadron B, 3rd The King's Own Hussars.

Infantry:

- 27th New Zealand Machine Gun Battalion. Lieutenant-Colonel F. J. Gwilliam.

4th New Zealand Infantry Brigade. Brigadier General James Hargest.

- Headquarters and Signal Section.
- 18th New Zealand Infantry Battalion.
- 19th New Zealand Infantry Battalion.
- 20th New Zealand Infantry Battalion.
- A section of machine gunners from the 27th New Zealand Machine Gun Battalion.

5th New Zealand Infantry Brigade. Brigadier General Hargest.

- Headquarters and Signal Section.
- 21st New Zealand Infantry Battalion.
- 22nd New Zealand Infantry Battalion.
- 23rd New Zealand Infantry Battalion.
- 28th (Maori) New Zealand Infantry Battalion.
- A section of machine gunners from the 27th New Zealand Machine Gun Battalion.
- 1st Regiment of Greek Infantry.

10th New Zealand Infantry Brigade. General Kippenberger.

- Headquarters and Signal Section.
- Oakes Force Composite Battalion (artillery and services used as infantry).
- 6th Regiment of Greek Infantry.
- 8th Regiment of Greek Infantry.
- Una sección de ametralladoras del 27th New Zealand Machine Gun Battalion.

Engineers:

- Commander Royal Engineers.
- 7th New Zealand Field Company (acting as infantry).
- 5th New Zealand Field Park Company.
- 19th Army Troops Company (acting as infantry).

Artillery:

- 1st Light Troop Royal Artillery (four 3.7 inch obuses).
- A section of the 256th Light Australian AA Battery (six 40 mm Bofors pieces).
- A section of the 7th Light Australian AA Battery (four 40 mm Bofors pieces).
- Section C of the Heavy AA Battery, Royal Marines (two 3 inch pieces).
- Z Coast Defence Battery RM (two 4 inch pieces).
- Section of the 23rd Light AA Battery RM (machine guns).
- 5th New Zealand Field Regiment (nine 75 mm pieces and two 3.7 inch pieces).

Royal Armoured Corps:

- Eight Mk VI cruiser tanks from the 3rd Hussars.
- Two *Matilda* Mk II infantry tanks from the 3rd Hussars.
- Two Mk VI light tanks from the 7th RTR.

Services:

- 5th New Zealand Field Ambulance.
- 6th New Zealand Field Ambulance.
- 4th New Zealand Field Hygiene Section.
- 7th British General Hospital.
- New Zealand Dental Corps.
- Deputy Assistant Director of Ordnance Services. Máleme Sector.
- Supply Column.

Another model of British tank present on Crete in May 1941 was the Mk. II (A10) cruiser tank..
lArtwork: Julio López Caeiro.

evacuation of the British and Allied troops and civilians, if the Germans achieved their objective.

With this framework, Freyberg confronted the long days at the end of May that were awaiting him.

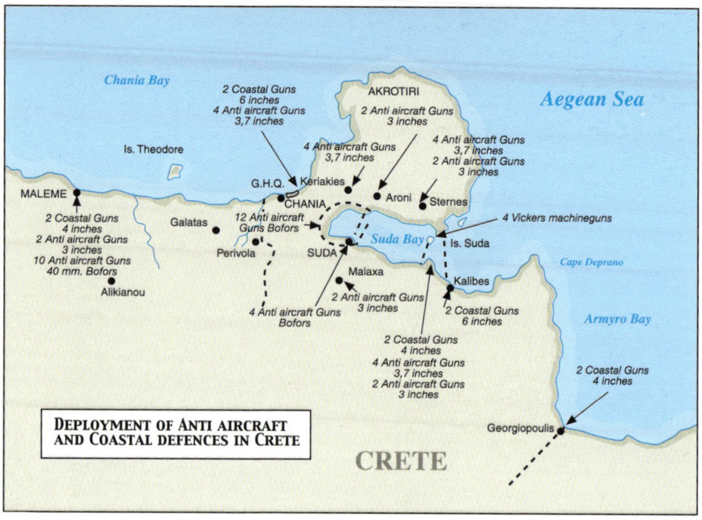

Emplacement of a coastal battery consisting in six inch pieces pertaining to the 15th Coast Artillery Regiment, in Souda Bay. (IWM HU60349).

A 40 mm L/60 Bofors anti-aircraft piece, manned by a mixture of British and Greek troops. The Allied troops unloaded thirty-six units of this magnificent cannon of Swedish origin on Crete. (IWM E1172).

Artwork: Julio López Caeiro.

CHAPTER IV ELEVEN DAYS OF COMBAT

Operation *«Mercury»* lasted for eleven days, in which the actions characterised by one side or another, as well as their outcome, allow us to split them into three concrete periods.

During the first three days, the operations carried out by the German paratroopers were authentic disasters, with the sole exception of those conducted at Maleme. In these first days, the results were so dreadful, with an incredibly high number of losses, as well as missed targets, that any other army would have aborted the operation. At sea, the situation was not much better, as on the night of the 22nd to 23rd, disaster struck one of the

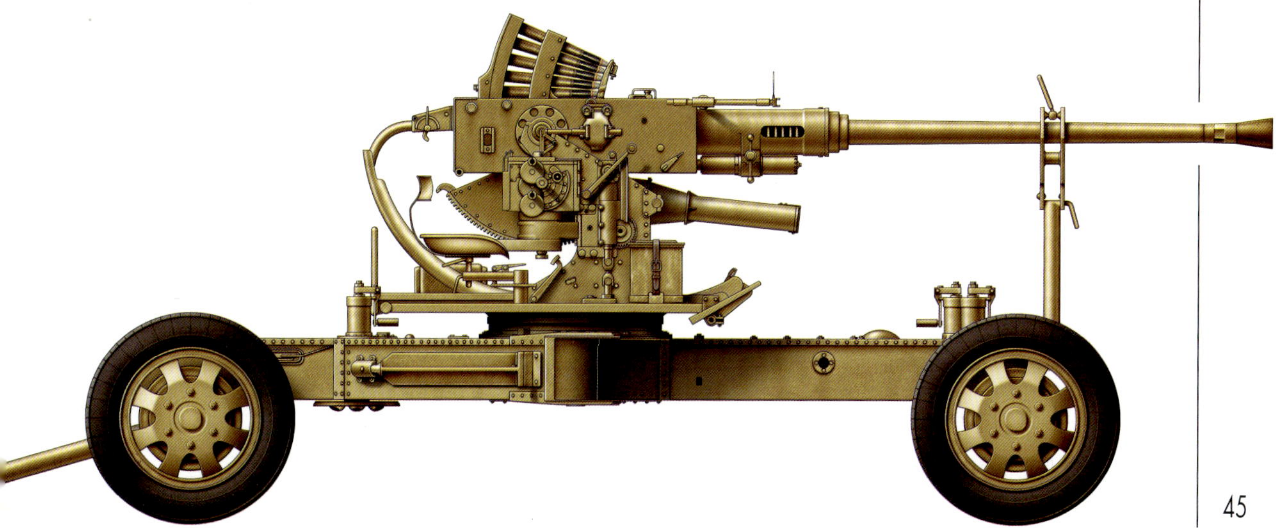

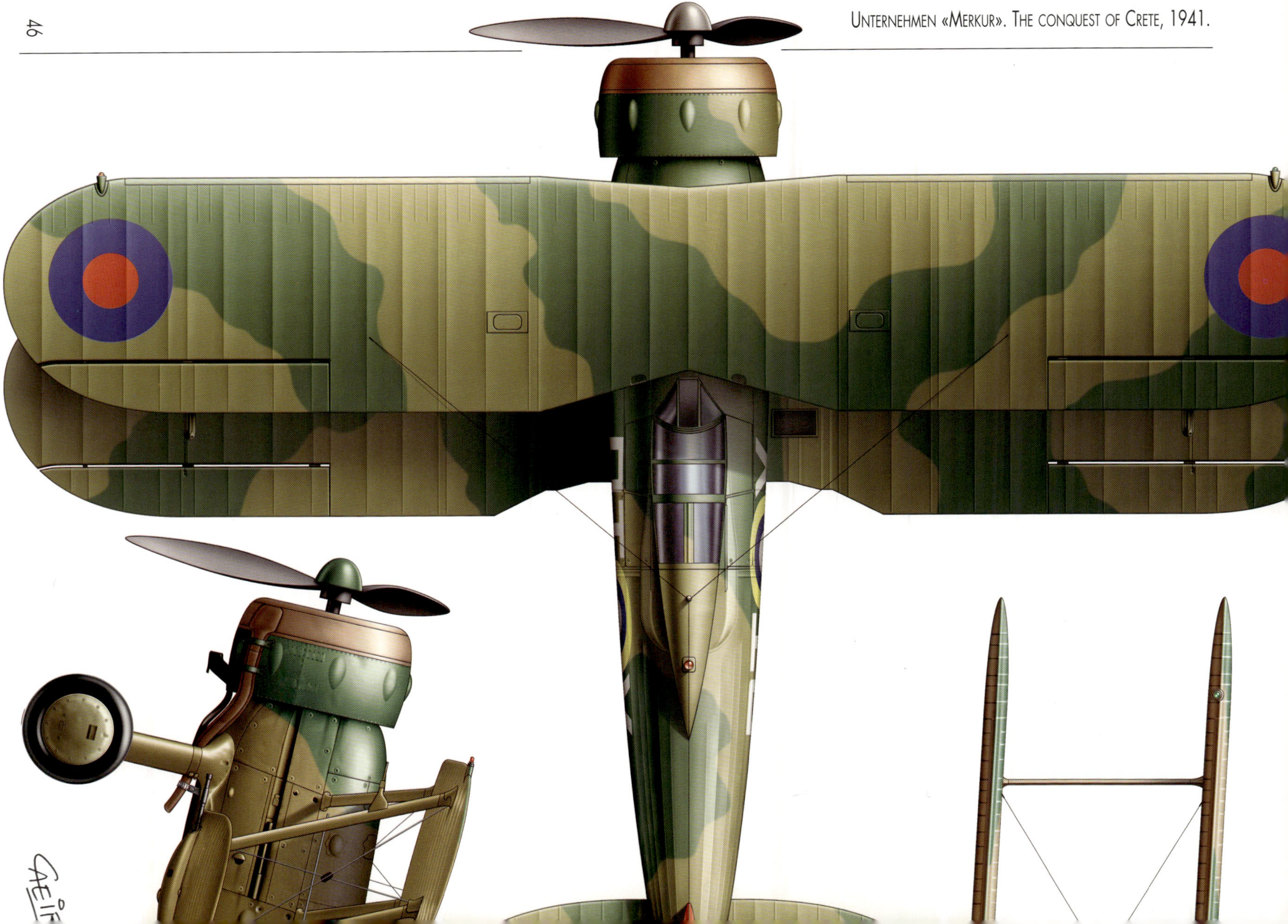

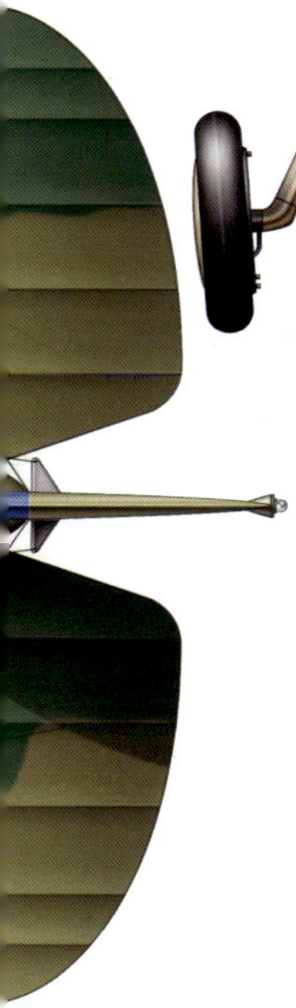

On the 19th of May, the scarce aeroplanes of the Royal Air Force and Fleet Air Army remaining on the island left Crete, including the twelve Gloster *Gladiator* Mk.II of the 112th Squadron. However, not all of them managed to escape, as several were machine-gunned by *Luftwaffe* fighters while on the ground, the remains of which were found on the Maleme runways after the invasion.

Artworks: Julio López Caeiro.

THE ROYAL AIR FORCE AND FLEET AIR ARM IN CRETE

Air Officer Commander-in-Chief, Middle East, Air Chief Marshall Sir Arthur Longmore
Airfields: Heraklion and Maleme

Unit	**Command**	**Planes**[1]
30th Squadron	*Sqn.Ldr.* R.A.Milward/*Sqn.Ldr.* Shannon	12 Bristol *Blenheim*
33rd Squadron	*Sqn.Ldr.* M.T.St.J Prattle *Sqn.Ldr.* Edward Howell, OBE, DFC	6 Hawker *Hurricane*
80th Squadron	*Sqn.Ldr.* E.G.Jones	Hawker *Hurricane*
112nd Squadron	*Sqn.Ldr.* L.G.Schwab	12 Gloster *Gladiator,* 2 Hawker *Hurricane*
805th FAA Squadron		6 Gloster *Sea Gladiator* 2 Fairey *Fulmar* ? Brewster *Buffalo*

1 Minimum quantities reflected in known reports.
2 Six *Hurricane* fighter planes between two squadrons.

The Hawker *Hurricane* Mk.I, with registration number W9298 was the last plane to leave Crete heading for Egypt, taking off on the 19th of May, piloted by Sergeant Maurice Bennett.
Artwork: Julio López Caeiro.

The Brewster *Buffalo* Mk.I from the 805 Squadron of the FAA with registration number AS420 left the Maleme airfield seriously damaged.
Artwork: Luis Fresno Crespo.

convoys that was transporting the mountain troops and equipment heading for the island. However, from the second day, Generaloberst Student took the reins of the unfortunate situation, opting to secure a single target and then he allowed himself to obtain the rest. Furthermore, he assumed the direct command of his men, supporting them and providing them with the necessary morale so that they would grow before the adverse situation. The result of his implication was, above all, the adaptability of his men to the adverse situation, which did not happen on the other side, as the British were very strict in their actions, not departing from the script imposed on them for anything. Definitively, the British were incapable of adapting to the variations of the events that the Germans introduced gradually.

Then, from the fourth day onwards, the situation changed through different actions, like the confrontation in the town of Galata, which occurred on the night of 24th to 25th, and which managed to tip the balance in favour of the Germans. From this moment, the Allied forces gave the battle up for lost and decided to organise their flight, more than a retreat as such, from the island. By the 31st, they had managed to evacuate the majority of their forces and the "guests" of other nationalities who were with them on Crete.

AAlthough we will later examine in detail the development of events, broadly speaking, events unfolded as follows: The attack on Crete began in the early hours of the 20th May 1941; two main waves of attack were made on four targets, with three different attack groups, the west, centre and east. The central group also had to cover two different targets distanced far apart. Having initially failed to achieve either of them, it was obliged to focus on a single action. This was, according to General Student's judgement, the only target that could possibly be taken in the whole of the action being carried out. He intended to take a bridgehead that would ser-

November 1940, Souda Bay: Greek and British troops fraternising around the omnipresent packet of cigarettes. (IWM E1177).

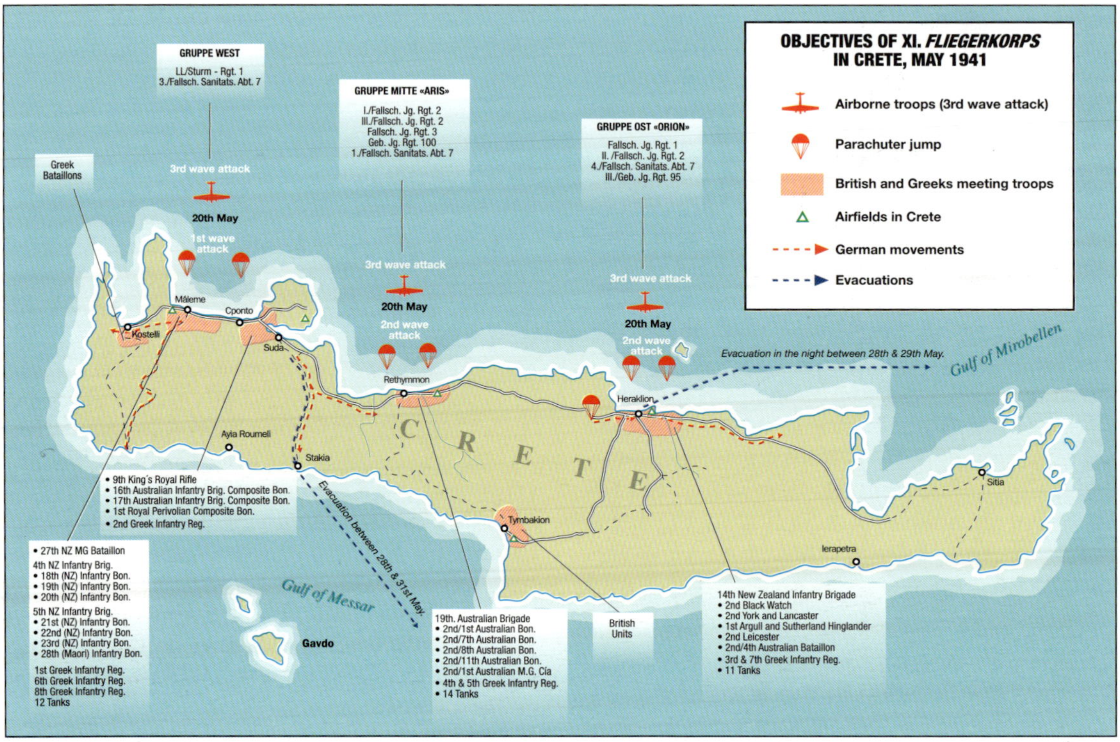

ve to attack other points, in which some of the units dropped the on first day were still involved. Finally, all the targets were taken and the attack on the rest of the island began, firstly eastwards and then southwards. However, the lack of good roads and the work of the British commandos, who landed on Crete for this purpose half-way through the battle, prevented the British from being "surrounded" and more than ten thousand managed to escape via the sea. Also, the Cretan guerrilla (who more than a simple guerrilla, carried out a typical labour of uncontrolled elements, in fact, truly delinquent) with the blessing of the British, postponed, but did nor prevent, the conquest of the island after "the eleven very long days of May".

DIFFICULT DAYS FOR THE GERMANS

The eve

The *Luftwaffe* sent all its available bombers in Greece for the attack. The large-scale "softening" actions tend to be very useful for destroying the defences of positions to be attacked, but curiously, this was not the case in Crete, basically due to the inaccuracy of the information available. On the other hand, an undesirable effect may result, as was the case, warning that an attack would be made shortly afterwards.

The British assessed the results of the waves of bombardment and rapid machine-gunning and discovered that the damage to human forces (dead and wounded) had been minimal, as well as the destructions of the defence mechanisms, which had been raised around the fields over the past six weeks. In the majority of cases, these had been erected with elements found near the targets to be defended and hence, with a temporary or circumstantial idea of protection. Thus, the damage produced was easily reparable in a matter of hours. However, luck was on the German side. Almost by chance, while the bombardments did not affect the artillery positions, they were very effective on the telephone lines and radio stations, as well as the communications

Following page, above: The *Luftwaffe* dropped all the forces available in continental Greece on the island. In the snapshot, a formation of Junkers Ju 88 is flying over the island. (Bundesarchiv 101-528-2374).

Following page, below: The port installations in Souda Bay and ships anchored there, after the passage of a wave of Junkers Ju 87 Stuka dive bombers. (IWM E3138).

routes. The few hits were probably pure luck, but in any case, they were very effective, as the British Achilles heel was the lack of infrastructure on the island. Crete did not have an adequate communications network, not only of roads of any kind, but its telephone network was perhaps the worst of all, which the bombers damaged very particularly. This left different British and Greek positions isolated from the rest of the battle, because the flexibility of ideas amongst the British command was practically non-existent. The British commands only fulfilled orders from above; if they failed to arrive, they continued with the original plan, without any variations. This was suicidal, when the other side prioritised improvisation, due to the fact that from the first moment, they were unable to achieve any of their initial objectives. The only positive factor for avoiding its destruction, was the order to retreat received by the scarce British aerial forces present.

In the early hours of the 20th May 1941, the sky of Crete was populated with parachutes (Bundesarchiv 183-L22010).

20th May 1941: The attack begins.

The *Gruppe West*: Attacking Maleme

While it was still night, the first Junker aeroplanes and gliders they were towing took off on course for Crete. Their target was Maleme, to take the aerodrome, survey the zone in detail towards the southeast and unite the *Fallschirmjäger Regiment* 3 in the zone of Chania with the eastern first wave of the *Gruppe Mitte*, near Souda Bay. At the crack of dawn, a new German bombardment attacked the places where the action was to develop, but with very poor results. Shortly afterwards, the slow transport aeroplanes towing the gliders appeared on the horizon. At 06:45 hours, now with the light of day, the first Junkers were greeted with very strong anti-aircraft fire and the first gliders fell to the ground at their targets. The Flieger were unaware that below them, the men of the 5th New Zealand Infantry Brigade were awaiting them, together with the 21st, 22nd, 23rd and 28th Maori Battalions, supported by an engineer unit and five field artillery and anti-aircraft units. The Junkers, in a "V" formation, started to release the gliders to immediately begin dropping the paratroopers

The bridge over the River Tavronitis was the target of the 4th Section of the *3./ Luftlande Sturmregiment.*

at a very low altitude. The sky was filled with the white and green parachutes used by the troops and the chestnut or grey-green of those from which the containers carrying the arms were suspended. The sub-waves within the main wave were separated by periods of fifteen minutes and this managed to increase the dispersion of the attackers even further, combined with the anti-aircraft fire and strong winds.

The luck of the battalions was very different in terms of the problems they faced but very similar in terms of the disaster they were confronted with, practically as soon as they stepped out of their aeroplanes. About half a dozen gliders per company, landed on different fixed objectives, in some cases correctly, but in others they were greatly off-course.

The General Staff and the First Battalion of the *Luftlande Sturmregiment* landed aboard its gliders in a precise manner, at the mouth of the River Tavronitis, to the west of the aerodrome, although at that point, it only existed in name and the river was actually more of a winter or occasional torrent than a river as such. The targets were as follows: The road, which joined the extremities of the island from east to west and a bridge of almost seventy metres long over the dry riverbed. The bridge was one of the most important targets to take and above all, they were to prevent it from being blown-up by the defenders. To the south of the road was Hill 107, which overlooked the riverbed, the road, and above all, the aerodrome runways. The rocky ground of which the dry riverbed was constituted had already been responsible for the first losses and a small cloud of dust slightly occulted the 22nd New Zealand Infantry Battalion from view, positioned at Hill 107, which opened machinegun fire on them even before they landed. The commander of the headquarters combat unit, Major Braun, was lost during these first moments, together with many other men.

It was seven o'clock in the morning and the following units of the first battalion began to land around the hill on the western side, from where the intense New Zealand fire resulted in countless losses among the paratroopers, including Major Walter Koch

Glider No. 16 posing (so to speak) near the bridge over the Tavronitis, in dip in the road to Kastelli.

(the hero of Eben Emael) who was seriously wounded in the head and Hauptman Sarrazin, commander of the 4th company, who was fatally hit. While the 3rd company commanded by Oberleutnant Von Plessen managed to "position" seven of his gliders at the position of the anti-aircraft pieces at Maleme, from where there was an attempt at hand-to-hand combat during the first moments. The last paratroopers landed in the midst of the clamour of the combat and shots were fired at them from Hill 107; it was 07:15 hours.

At 07:30 hours, at the orders of Major Otto Scherber, the III./LLStR. landed at Hill 107. Meanwhile, much further to the west, the II./LLStR. landed, under the command of Major Edgar Stenzler, to constitute the operations reserve. Only its 6th company entered into direct action, its mission being to take the Kastelli Bridge. Meanwhile the IV./LLStR., commanded by Hauptman Walter Gericke, together with the medical company and regimental logistics, landed together at the town of Tavronitis, accompanied by *Generalmajor* Eugen Meindl in person.

In this photograph taken on the 21st June 1941, we can see Major Walter Koch, the hero of Eben Emael, still convalescing from the serious wounds received at Hill 107, ready to board the aeroplane that would repatriate him to Germany. (Bundesarchiv 146-2006-0084).

Chaos around Maleme!

To the north of the bridge and near the machine gun niches next to the aerodrome, *Oberfelwebel* Arpke led his men to their targets by hand grenade hits. None of the gliders had landed at the right place and one of them had even failed to land on Crete, but rather on Antykhitera, an island situated to the north of the path from the continent.

Some classes of troops were forced to take control of their sections, as was the case for *Oberjäger* Erich Schuster, who took two Bofors cannons from those that had hit the other companies. Meanwhile, *Oberleutnant* Von Plessen, in command of his company, the 3rd, tried to capture other Bofors cannons before dying.

The losses were terrible, but they managed to capture more pieces of artillery. All the offi-

Hauptman Walter Gericke, commander of the *IV./LLStR.*, photographed in July 1941, shortly after being decorated with the *Ritterkreuzes zum Eisernen Kreuz.* (16/7/1941).

The DFS 230 attack gliders could accommodate one pilot and nine equipped soldiers in the DFS 230A-1 variant and two pilots and 8 soldiers in the DFS 230A-2 version with dual command. In total, 1,593 units were built by Ghota, Erla and Hartwig and another 410 in Czechoslovakia. (Bundesarchiv 141-0816).
Artwork: Julio López Caeiro.

cers of arms had died and medical officer *Oberartz* Weisel had assumed command of the company.

At the other end of the coast and the road, the 4th company was also in the midst of the chaos. In this case, the succession of command had been conferred to *Stabsarzt Jäger*, who had managed to entrench himself at the foot of Hill 107. His situation was desperate, but the 13th, 14th and 15th companies of *Hauptman* Walter Gericke's IV./LLStR. came to their assistance.

Junkers Ju 87 B *Stuka* bombarded companies C and D of the 22nd New Zealand Infantry Battalion; whose commander, Colonel Andrew was unaware of the situation, as he had lost radio communications and had no messengers to inform him. Neither did he receive orders from his superior, Brigadier James Hargest. Company C, under the command of Captain Jonson, began ceding its positions to the south of the aerodrome and the end of the

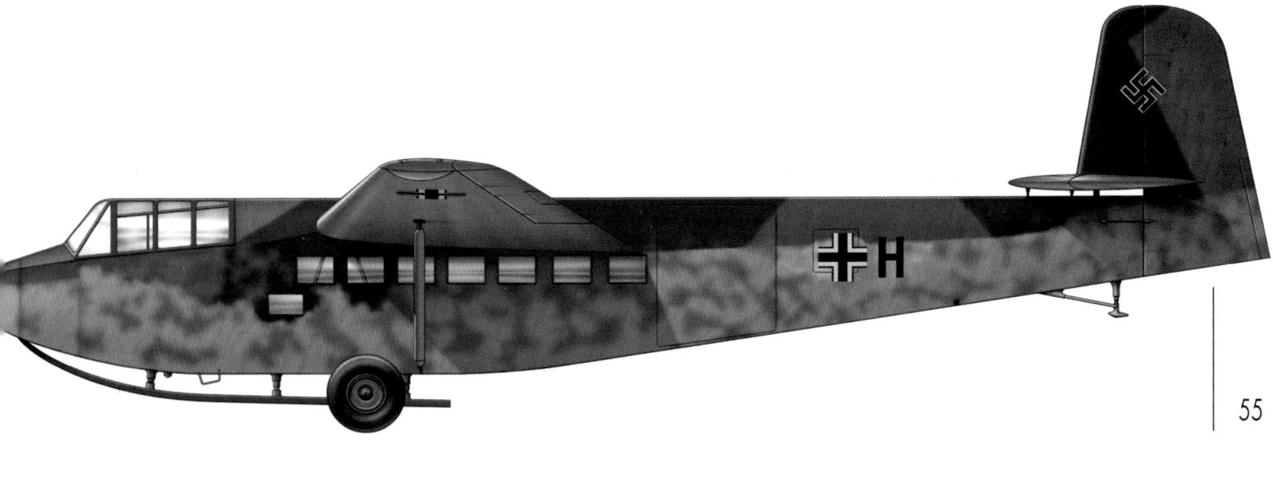

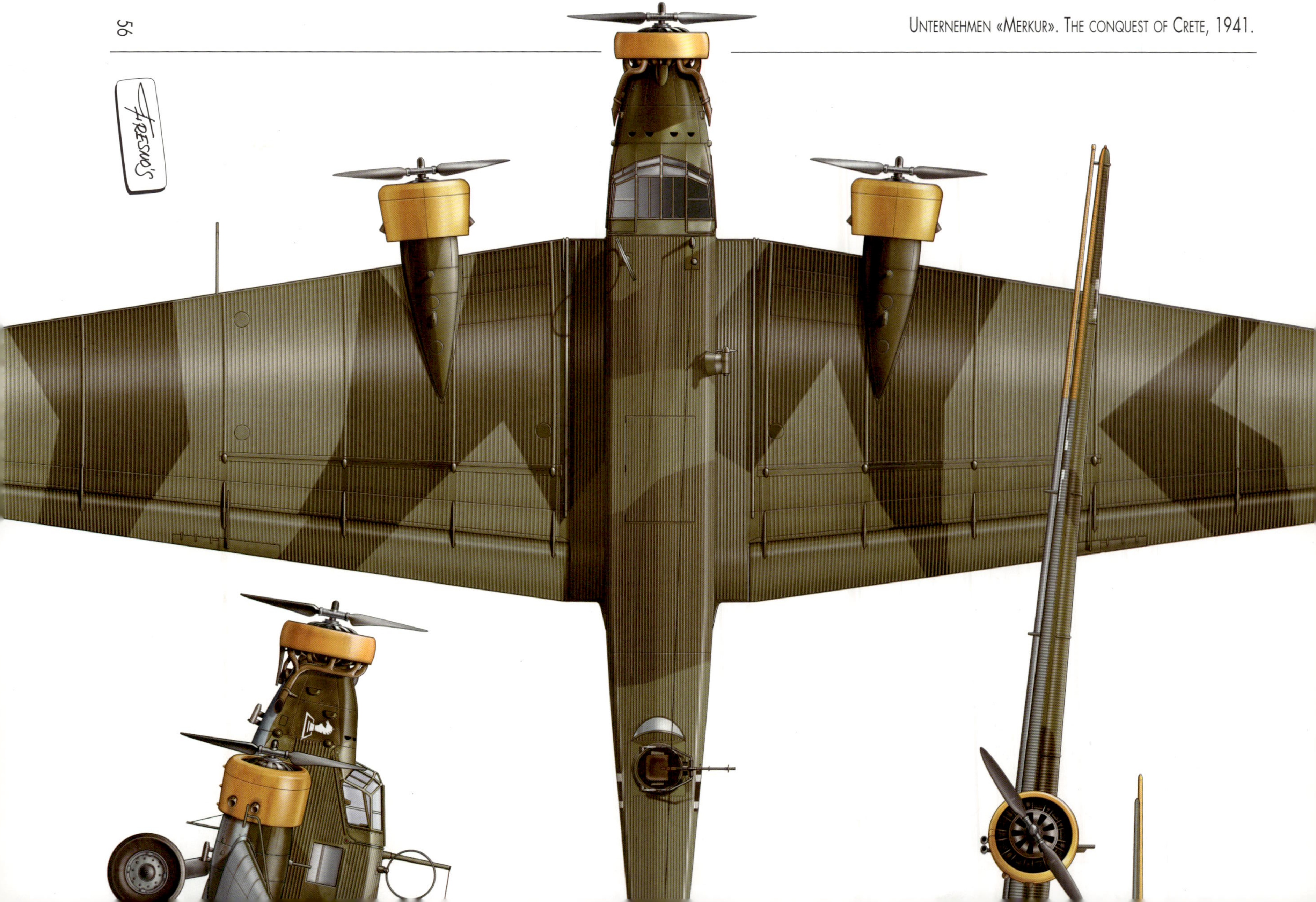
FRESNO'S

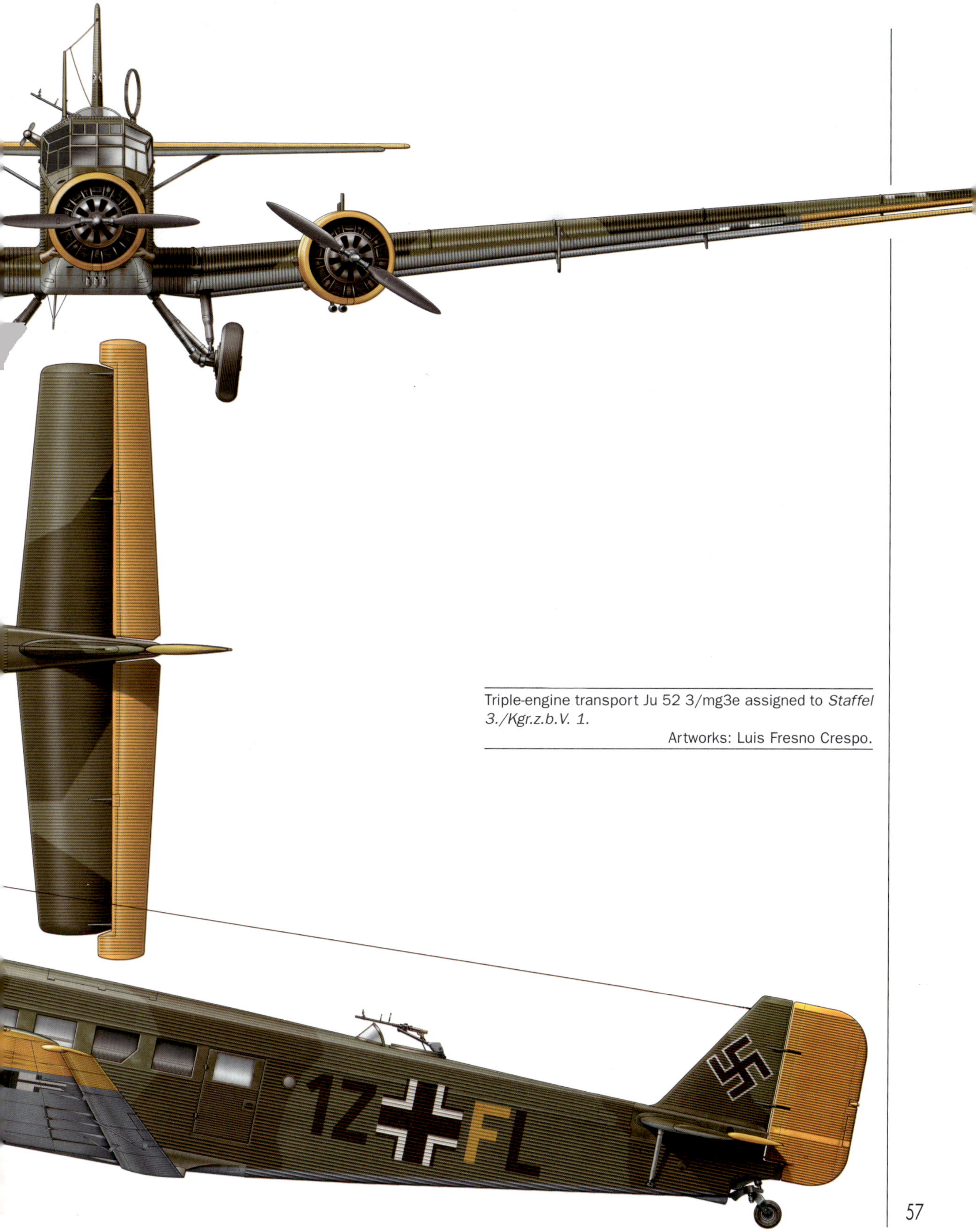

Triple-engine transport Ju 52 3/mg3e assigned to *Staffel 3./Kgr.z.b.V. 1.*

Artworks: Luis Fresno Crespo.

When the parachute drop began, the Ju 52 carrying elements of the *Fallschirmjäger Regiment 3* received accurate anti-aircraft fire which resulted in them being diverted from their targets and meant that the drop was inaccurate and greatly dispersed over an area more than five kilometres from where the drop should have taken place. In the following two photos, we can see a Ju 52 falling to the ground in flames, while four parachutes open at a low altitude (we don't know whether they were members of the crew or parachutists being transported). In the second photo, a dense column of smoke is rising up to the sky after the plane's impact and explosion, while the second Ju 52 leaves a trail of parachutists behind it and the aforementioned parachutists are about to touch ground. (IWM A4144 y 4145).

highway. The 3rd German company was pressuring them severely and, supported by Braun's men, they managed to take the administrative zone that the Royal Air Force had set up there, to the south of the aerodrome. Jonson asked for the support of tanks in reserve, but Colonel Andrew denied his request.

The morning progressed between attacks and counter-attacks from one side or the other. At midday, Colonel Andrew lost his temper due to a lack of information and launched the white and green flares that gave the order to the 23rd Battalion to support the rearguard line. They didn't even move. Later on, they were pleased not to have seen the signal. From midday onwards, the Germans had managed to position mortars and a piece of artillery and began to beat the enemy's devices. At 17:00 hours, Andrew once again asked for communications to be re-established with Brigadier Hargest. He communicated that the 23rd New Zealand Infantry Battalion was involved in another fight and that he could not send it. This was not true, but Andrew, who was unaware of this, decided to counterattack with the two Matilda (from the 7th Royal Tank Regiment) he had at his disposition and a group of volunteers. The first tank went over an embankment, just before reaching the Tavronitis Bridge; the other one turned back, because its tower was "jammed". The infantry accompanying them suffered hard losses as they retreated, having been left without the protection of the two tanks.

Chania (Canea), the Maleme flank

As with Maleme, the plans to take Chania were excessively optimistic. To this was added the organised defence of the British, which in this case consisted in the 4th New Zealand Infantry Brigade and two Greek battalions.

Two companies of the *LLStR.*, which together were known as the *Kampfgruppe Altmann,* landed in their gliders near the headquarters of the CREOFORCE, immediately after it had been machine-gunned by German Messerschmitt Bf

The aerial attack by the Fallschirmjäger did not manage to surprise the Commonwealth troops, which were perfectly entrenched... (IWM E32025E).

... and from their positions, they inflicted great mortality on the German paratroopers as they landed. (Bundesarchiv 101-166-0527-10a y 22).

CIORDIA

109's and Bf 110's. Its target was a false artillery position, which was in fact the trenches of the Northumberland Hussars. The landing was followed by fire from the British machine guns, which resulted in 108 dead and wounded from the 138 men of the second company of paratroopers. Practically all the survivors were taken prisoner, among them, Altmann himself, the hero of Eben Emael. The first company was not so lucky, as its target (this one real) was four 3.7 inch pieces, attended by 180 men and several machine guns. After the perfect landing of all the gliders except two, the strong reaction of the entrenched British forced the paratroopers to retreat, until they reached an appropriate place to take shelter and await reinforcements, while they were being besieged by the New Zealanders.

Meanwhile, the men of the *Fallschirmjäger Regiment 3* had even worse luck, if possible. When the parachute jump had begun, the Ju 52 received the dense anti-aircraft fire that forced them to deviate from their targets and meant that the drop was imprecise and highly dispersed over an area of more than five kilometres from where they should have been dropped. In fact, they landed directly on the 10th New Zealand Infantry Brigade, part of the 4th New Zealand Infantry Brigade and the Greek battalions. They were shot during the descent or as soon as they touched the ground, many of them dying or being wounded. This was the first drop of many that would later repeat the same pattern. Contravening the Geneva Convention, the British troops carried out highly censurable acts, firing at defenceless paratroopers, or killing the wounded and allowing the Cretan civilians to finish off the wounded Germans and then loot their bodies.

In any case, not all the units had the same bad luck. The worst off were the members of the III Battalion, who fell in the midst of the New Zealand positions, and the support company, which completely fell in a lake, where the majority of its men drowned. The I Batta-

The Junkers Ju 52 3/mg3e were the *Luftwaffe's* standard aeroplane for the transport of paratroopers. This type of aeroplane could carry 18 equipped paratroopers, for 1,290 km. From top to bottom:

- Machine belonging to the *Stab IV./Kgr.z.b.V. 1.* It still bore traces of its pre-war camouflage.
- Junkers Ju 52 3/mg3e of the *1./Kgr.z.b.V. 105.*
- Junkers Ju 52 3/mg3e of the *5./Kgr.z.b.V. 106.*

Artwors: Luis Fresno Crespo.

1Z BF

G6 DX

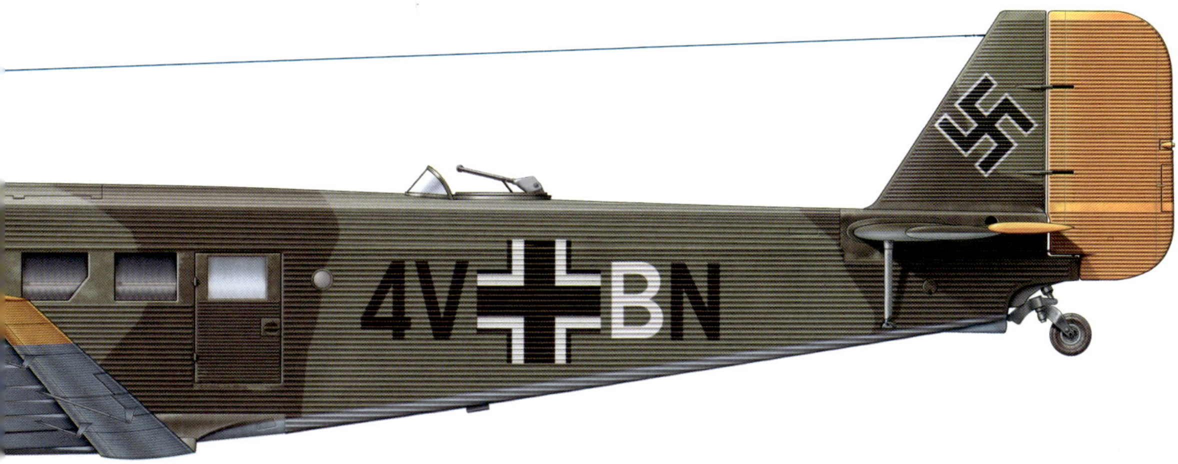
4V BN

lion had similar luck and accidentally almost managed to capture the King of Greece, by landing between Chania and Aliaknou, very close to the place where the royal entourage was located. King George II of Greece was in a villa owned by Enmanouil Tsouderos, near Perivolia, and not very far from Chania. The security personnel assigned to the King were able to observe how the paratroopers fell barely metres from the fences of the residence and how they fought with a New Zealand unit that was protecting the surrounding area. Faced with the imminent problems, the British liaison officer, Lieutenant Colonel W. H. Ryan and the chief of the Cretan police, who were in the villa, decided to evacuate the King and his entourage: George II, his cousin Peter, Colonel M. Levidis (the King's master of ceremonies), Mr Tsouderos and Kyriakos Varvaressos (governor of the Bank of Greece). In his precipitated flight, the King forgot some vitally important papers and while the entourage continued the journey south, his assistant tried to return to the house. It was impossible, as the Germans had already taken the building and were fighting the New Zealanders in the gardens and surrounding areas. During their flight, the entourage was mistaken by the irregular Cretan soldiers for disguised Germans and they were forced to spend the night at Therisso. Finally, once matter had been resolved, they reached the south coast, boarding the H.M.S. *Decoy* together with British diplomatic personnel and they reached Alexandria during the night of the 22nd.

Landing accidentally in such a strongly guarded and defended zone was like falling into a trap, as many paratroopers were killed, wounded and taken prisoner right at the start of the action and shortly afterwards, the majority of its members met with a similar fate. The II Battalion fell to the north of the highway, in the Galatas zone. Only the companies of sappers and one other isolated section fell in peaceful zones, were able to collect their weapons from the containers and regroup to efficiently attack the 6th Battalion of Greek Infantry, which then fled. They equally managed to surprise and destroy a battery deployed at the foot of Mount Daratros.

The elements that fell in the Galatas zone met with the presence of three Mk VI light tanks, commanded by Lieutenant Farran,

which attacked them as they landed, preventing them from regrouping and recovering their heavy weaponry that had been dropped in the containers. The British tank drivers committed the injustice of firing at the surrendering paratroopers and allowed the Cretan civilian population to savagely murder the mounded and loot the dead.

The prison at Ayia (Agia)

No everything ended in disaster, as some of the men from the I and II Battalions managed to regroup around Oberst Richard Heydrich, commander of the *Fallschirmjäger Regiment 3,* who led them to Ayia. This officer had become the highest ranking German officer of the division, as his immediate superior, *Generalleutnant* Willhelm Süssman, had fallen with his glider on the island of Egina, when the towing cable broke. During the difficult landing, the commander and four men from his General Staff died.

At Ayia (Agia), its old prison was about to enter the pages of history. This old building, built from stone blocks, with an unbroken and strong wall around it, also made of stone, became the ideal place for defensive action. About a thousand paratroopers took refuge in the building, which was also equipped with water reserves and an abandoned hospital that was quickly put into service. The occupation of this building was one of the numerous failed tactics of the British, who should have taken the building in foresight. They were quickly surrounded by their pursuers, two Greek battalions and another couple of New Zealand ones, which were later assisted by other units. The Allies launched an attack on the old prison, but the fort resisted, as was to be expected. This marked a moment of tranquillity and rest on both sides, but it prevented the German progression towards Chania.

At midday, the situation could not have been worse. Not one single objective of the West Group had been attained: Maleme, Canea, Hill 107, etc. The majority of the troops had landed far away from their targets, at sea, on the nearby islands, or what was worse, on or near the Allied units, which were found perfectly entrenched and who from their positions, had caused a great loss of life among the German paratroopers. This had resulted in the death of a very significant number of Fallschirmjäger and above all, of numerous officers of arms, which obliged many logistics officers or non-commissioned officers to assume command of the combats. In addition to all this, the most important formation comprising almost a thousand men was surrounded in the prison of Ayia, with no possibility of freeing themselves.

All of these extremes were so unknown to Generaloberst Kurt Student, that on the Greek peninsular, he barely received information about what was happening. The pilots who returned informed that the objectives were being met, though with the loss of numerous aeroplanes, knocked down by the anti-aircraft weapons, but with no other news. Re-provisioning, as we have already mentioned, became very complicated. Dense clouds of dust followed the landings in Greece, which impeded the effective manipulation of the aeroplanes by the ground personnel. Also, having to refill the tanks manually slowed down the preparation of the second wave. The delay in conditioning and refuelling meant that the aeroplanes left more slowly and consequently, the drops also took more time. Furthermore, this delay enabled the anti-aircraft defences to be warned and prepared for the following waves of paratroopers.

The *Gruppe Mitte*

Its first target was the aerodrome of Rethymno, to then head westwards to attack and take Souda Bay.

The delay caused by decanting the fuel postponed the departure time to 13:30 hours. After three and a half hours flight, the 1,800 *Fallschirmjäger* of the FJR 2, commanded by *Oberst* Alfred Sturm, commenced their descent over the targets, but the intense anti-aircraft fire dispersed the slow triple engine Junkers Ju 52. Of the 160 taking part, seven were knocked down. The paratroopers fell directly over the two Greek and two Australian battalions that were defending the positions. Devastating fire resulted in multiple wounds. On top of this, there was the problematic terrain: Very arid, very rocky, with vineyards, olives and scrub, which resulted in wounds upon arrival to the ground.

When they attempted to regroup, they were attacked by the two *Matilda* Mk.II infantry tanks and were subjected to fire from six 75 mm pieces. Also, the infantry of the 19th Australian Brigade, commanded by Lieutenant Colonel I. R. Campbell, rapidly launched an attack on them. Amidst the chaos, the I and III Battalions managed to capture both hills of vineyards and olives that were housing Allied artillery pieces and machine guns, taking shelter there, as progression in any direction was impossible. Small groups were attacked by a large number of Cretan civilians, who killed and looted them. Some sections managed to regroup and established strongholds in two towns: Perivolia and Stavromenos, where they decided to fight until they were rescued or perished.

The *Gruppe Ost.*

Heraklion was being defended by the 14th British Infantry Brigade (Black Watch, Leicester and York & Lancaster's), supported by several Greek units. They had several batteries of anti-aircrafts Bofors (twelve cannons in total), which were very well camouflaged and had remained intact after the attacks by the bombers and later machine-gunning by the German fighters.

Oberst Alfred Sturm (awarded the *Ritterkreuzes zum Eisernen Kreuz* on the 9/7/1941), was commanding the *Fallschirmjäger Regiment 2*, on the 20th May 1941. (Bundesarchiv 146-2006-0090).

The men of the *Fallschirmjäger Regiment* 1 began dropping around the city and airport. These were their main targets in addition to the port where the mountain troops were to land, who were heading there in a maritime convoy. To the east, the III Battalion was dropped, while the I Battalion did so to the west and south, with reinforcements from two companies of the FJR 2. The 6th and 7th companies that landed to the west of the aerodrome were annihilated. Devastating anti-aircraft fire decimated the paratroopers and the aeroplanes transporting them, although without reaching the figure of losses at Chania and Rethymno. Oberst Bruno Bräuer, commander of the *Fallschirmjäger Regiment 1*, faced with the impossibility of taking the aerodrome, opted for regrouping his forces and making strongholds in the nearby buildings that had not been occupied by the British. They observed the lack of fire power and almost immediately attacked the exposed paratroopers,

The *III./FJR 1*, commanded by *Major* Kart-Lothar Schultz, barely suffered any losses during the airdrop from the Ju 52 triple-engine planes, was easily able to pick up the collective weapons from the containers and it prepared to take the town of Heraklion. (Bundesarchiv 183-L19105).

The narrow lanes of Heraklion bore witness to bloody combats.

without taking any precautions, but they did not always come off so well. The hardened German troops, assisting one another, repelled many of these attacks, especially when the Australians placed themselves between the two lines of fire.

Taking refuge in the buildings was a success and they managed to repel the attacks made by the British with the support of the two *Matilda* Mk.II tanks and Mk.VI light tanks.

Major Kart-Lothar Schultz, commander of the III Battalion, managed to regroup his men who had barely suffered any losses and stormed the city that was being defended by a Greek police unit of eighty men. The 15th Century Venetian wall was unable to keep out the *Fallschirmjäger* who took a sector of the wall and the Chania gate. The German tactical superiority overcame political resistance, in a hard and bloody battle that forced the Mayor of Heraklion to surrender the city. But the Germans' joy did not last for long. The Australians attacked the city and the Germans, clearly outnumbered, decided to retreat to better positions, until night fell, the moment chosen by the German commanders, due to their superior tactical military training, to attack the aerodrome of Heraklion and the city with its port.

Heraklion retained part of the wall, in which the west gate can be seen.

Dusk on the first day of operations.

EIn Athens, *Generalmajor* Kurt Student, began to receive real information about what was happening. The radio gradually provided small reports of the losses that had resulted and although they were not as severe as the actual situation, they provided the German commander with a pessimistic perspective on what was happening.

By mid-afternoon, none of the targets on the island had been attained and many commanders and officers had died. The majority of the groups, formed from the survivors, were found taking refuge on the defensive and very few were in a position to carry out nocturnal attacks to try and obtain any beneficial target. A notable delay had occurred in the landing of mountaineers in the first fleet of caiques and their arrival at the island was going to be delayed significantly, perhaps for more than 24 hours. Although, this didn't bear much importance, as there was no beach or port where they could land.

General Student revised the situation with his General Staff, deciding to reinforce the attack on Maleme. At that point, they believed it to be the only possible target from which to continue the attack and the only one where the planned intentions could be obtained. If they were wrong, it would be a disaster and if it were not so, perhaps they would be able to take the island, although with a delay and great losses. For Student, Hill 107 was the key to the action and he hoped that somebody would manage to take it and above all, hold it. At Maleme, the situation was complicated in the eyes of Colonel Andrews and his decisions were to mark the future of the operations. Furthermore, a veteran from the "Condor Legion" was going to make Student happy.

Dusk at Maleme

Colonel Andrew believed it was impossible to maintain his positions. It was 18:00 hours and he informed the Brigade command that if he did not receive reinforcements, he would have to retreat to new positions. They replied to him, dodging the issue and informing him that two companies were going to reinforce him, which was not true. The decision was also placed in his hands with a cryptic sentence: "If you must do it, do it". Andrew, desperately decided to retreat. Due to the poor internal communications, companies C and D were not informed and, having not received the message, they retreated, observing the others abandon the line for new positions. Finally, a company from the 28th Maori Battalion and another from the 23rd Battalion arrived; by then it was early in the morning. These units were not familiar with the terrain, were lost and were about to be ambushed by the reduced German troops. With the reinforcements, a new line of defence was established one and a half kilometres to the east of the initial positions.

This retreat was one of the greatest mistakes committed by the Allies. Hill 107 was an important target to conquer, although it was initially not considered to be of any real value. It overlooked the aerodrome and hence was vital, both for defending it and attacking it. Furthermore, a four inch battery was established on the hill that was not being used by the British, due to the strictness of the orders, which assigned the battery to the coastal defence. It could only be used for this purpose and did not fire at infantry troops or other targets. Occasionally, the infantry asked for its support during the fighting against the paratroopers, but the commander of the gunners always refused.

Heroes

That night, the debated and argued action of Dr. Neumann was carried out. This *Oberstabsarzt*, (medical commander) of the Paratrooper Attack Regiment had already carved a history as a fearful fighter. Veteran of the "*Condor Legion*", he offered and occasionally managed to be a machine-gunner in the German bombers during the Spanish Civil War. Though this enormously raised the soldiers' morale, it was not to the liking of the superior commanders who thought that a living medical officer was worth more than a dead machine-gunner and they sent him back to Germany. On Crete, he once again proved his daring and bravery. There, he intervened as a commander of circumstance, due to the loss of the officers of arms during the attack and conquest of Hill 107 on the night of 20th to 21st. According to the German version, medical commander Neumann recruited fifteen paratroopers and led them in the attack uphill. After hard confrontations in the dark of the night and having one dead and several wounded, he managed to take the hillock and establish positions there. The aerodrome was at the mercy of German fire.

However, the British tried to play down the importance of the matter, stating that they were retreating from Hill 107 and that Neumann's men simply exchanged shots with the last New Zealanders to retreat. It is unknown which side was telling the truth, though it is likely to have been a mixture of both versions. Perhaps the combat took place during the final part of the British retreat and Neumann's men carried out a

Positioned on Hill 107, the Fallschirmjäger of the *LL-Sturm-Regt.* observe the Maleme aerodrome in the distance.

full-blown attack, though thinking that they would be repelled by the British. In the end, the situation did not prevent the hill from being taken before they abandoned it as planned. The truth is that commander Neumann received the Knight's Cross of the Iron Cross for his heroic behaviour.

The night on Crete

Night fell at Chania. In the distance, the combats could be made out, which lessened gradually, until the noise of the battle was extinguished by the silence of the night. At the small fronts, the soldiers on both sides prepared to spend the night. At the time, nocturnal combats were not very common, so the night represented a short break. Near Chania was the Valley of Ayia, where the largest paratrooper contingent had taken refuge in the old abandoned prison. "Prison valley", as it would be known henceforth, also prepared for the following day's combat. Meanwhile, at Heraklion, disconcertment was at its greatest on both sides. The night was used to lick the wounds and the sunrise gave the signal for the hostilities to begin.

CHAPTER V
THE MALEME OPTION

21st of May 1941

Day broke at Maleme. *Hauptmann* Walter Gericke, commander of the IV Battalion received from *Major* Edgar Stenzler, provisional commander of the regiment, the order to take control of the aerodrome. The 3rd and 4th companies of the I Battalion were to support him. Throughout the morning, 300 paratroopers were dropped near the aerodrome and over Pyrgos (to the east), to support the action of those who were already on the ground.

The British, aware of the situation, used the artillery from the naval units anchored at Souda Bay and the land-based batteries that were defending the coast. They began to bomb the German positions, but lacking observers to guide their fire, their possible precision became erratic. The German response, with the only cannon captured in working condition on Hill 107 and the Bofors cannons captured at the aerodrome, as well as the light mortars that they had brought to the island, managed to "hammer" the New Zealanders in the "line" they had established after their retreat. The Germans feared a counter-attack, but this did not take place.

At midday, a solitary Junker Ju 52 appeared in the sky, which approached the aerodrome, flying low. The solitary aeroplane passed over and then began the gliding path towards the aerodrome. The paratroopers launched flares to dissuade it from its action, because the aerodrome was not operative, as it was partially being subjected to British fire. The pilot changed course slightly and descended towards the adjoining beach, where it landed and rolled over the sand. It was rapidly unloaded and as many wounded as possible boarded the plane, among them, *General Major Eugen* Meindl, who had been wounded at the start of the operation. The Junger took off, with difficulty, due to the sand. It was the first machine to have carried out a complete aerial operation on Crete; later others would come to carry out a small aerial carrousel.

The German morale had climbed several points. The observers realised that there was an area where the British were not aiming, at the western end of the aerodrome. Once *General der Flieger* Kurt Student was informed, he sent *Hauptmann* Kleye to try and land their. The aeroplane, which was transporting weapons and ammunition managed to land. The most seriously wounded were loaded onto the plane. The runway was workable, though with some reserves. From 18:00 hours onwards, the British lines became more distanced and a continuous carrousel began, although not all the aeroplanes were able to leave afterwards. The damage to the runway and fire that some of the aeroplanes received during the landing prevented them from returning to the air on some occasions. The *Fallschirmjäger* decided to maintain the runway operative at any cost and thus, when a plane was damaged, it was removed from the runway with the help of the Bren Carrier captured in the aerodrome, although more damage was often caused in the manoeuvre than it had initially received.

The next German movements were: An attack on the New Zealand positions, as well as dropping paratroopers to the east of Maleme and Pyrgos, as mentioned previously. At about 14:00 hours, the *Luftwaffe* launched a massive

In the early afternoon of the 21st May, three hundred paratroopers were dropped to the east of Maleme and Pyrgos. (Bundesarchiv 141-0864).

aerial attack on the British positions. Its result was apparently good, but the reality was that it was only moderately effective. The paratrooper jumps commenced immediately, but as had happened the previous day with the III./LLStR, they were annihilated as they fell, in the zone of Pyrgos, over the 28th (Maori) Battalion and a unit of engineers. The land-based progression, however, which left the aerodrome simultaneously, surprised the British, who did not discover the attackers until they were practically upon them. The combats moved away from the aerodrome and the frontline was located in the town itself. There, the fight became bloodier and more desperate by the New Zealanders, who stopped the progress of the Germans beyond the town, momentarily saving Pyrgos. Nevertheless, and in spite of the control that the Germans exercised on the aerodrome, the British artillery continued sporadically firing at the runways.

At 16:00 hours, the German situation was extremely precarious. With barely any ammunition, under a blazing sun, with the reinforcements of just 300 men, who had arrived under the command of Oberst Ramcke during the course of the morning, the Germans feared a counter-attack that would put an end to all of them, but this did not occur. Like the night before, or indeed the very same day, the British were unaware of their superiority and let the moment during which the Germans were not pressuring them slip away. They were unable to detect from this break in the combat, the weakness of the paratroopers and their real situation.

In fact, their lack of vision was conditioned by the certainty that an amphibious attack would shortly take place. They knew that between two and three naval convoys were heading for the island and they thought it more appropriate to wait for them and fight them as they approached Crete. They were unaware that the Germans' main card was the paratroopers and that furthermore, General Student had decided to place all his bets on Maleme.

At 17:00 hours, the *100 Gebirgsjäger Regiment* (Regiment of Mountain Infantry) of the *5.Gebirgs-Division* (Mountain Division) began to land at the damaged aerodrome under the command of *Oberst* Willibald Ut. The airborne landing of the mountaineers was not unstoppable. 600 men arrived throughout the afternoon, as well as the water and ammunition that were so scarce. The wounded were

Mountain troops heading for Crete aboard Junkers Ju 52 transporters. At 18:00 hours on the 21st May, elements of the *100 Gebirgsjäger Regiment* began to land at the battered aerodrome. (Bundesarchiv 146-1981-159-22).

carried away on the return flight of the transport aeroplanes. As many as 20 aeroplanes managed to land at Maleme per hour. At this point, the destiny of Crete was being decided and the Germans were beginning to win.

That night, relying on the numerical superiority of men and artillery, as well as disposing of three cruise tanks, the British command decided to launch a timid though very accurate attack against the positions at Maleme and very particularly, against Hill 107. However, the poor organisation delayed the starting time by four hours and the members, who were not familiar with the terrain, got lost and ended up in completely wrong places. To round off the matter, two of the three tanks came into range of the Bofors cannons captured by the Germans, who put them to use immediately.

At Galatas and the prison at Agia, two other strong points, a stalemate occurred that day. The Germans' good tactical situation allowed them to maintain the positions conquered on the first day, but their lack of numbers did not permit them to attack the Allies that outnumbered them by four to one. The Allies could have attacked them, but decided not to do so and they only carried out timid attacks on the defensive positions in very concrete zones, almost as if they wanted to probe the situation. This lack of decision would shortly prove fatal to them.

Rethymno and Heraklion

At Rethymno, the forces of the FJR 2, two battalions that were greatly diminished by the losses, were totally surrounded. One of them had been forced to withdraw to the installations of an abandoned oil factory. It took refuge there temporarily, waiting to receive help. Meanwhile, the other one, which was isolated in the middle of the field, managed to make a stronghold in the outskirts of the town of Perivolia, on the road to Heraklion. Both remained isolated for several days. The Greek and British forces, comprising more than seven thousand men, carried out several attacks that were always repelled, even when they were conducted with strong artillery preparation, or the use of tanks. Finally, the advance of the troops that took Maleme managed to make contact with the isolated paratroopers at Rethymno, in a short period of time.

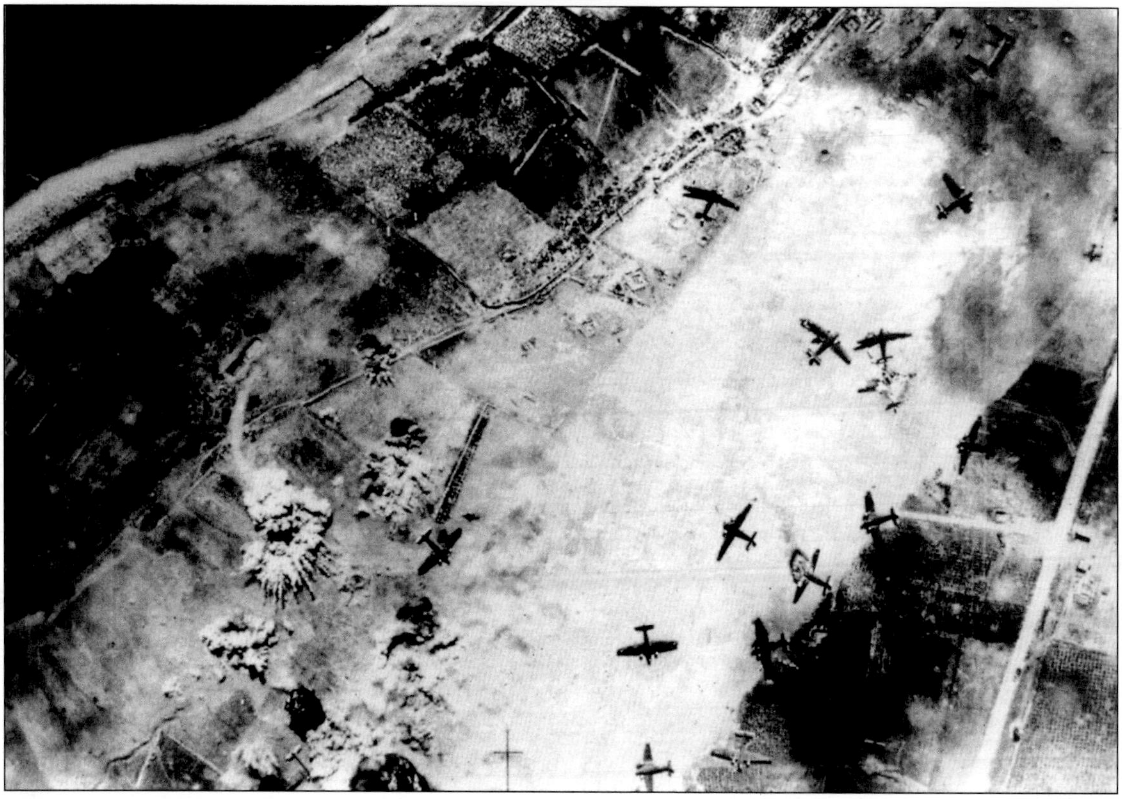

On the 21st, four battalions of *Gebirgsjäger*, led by the chief of division, *Generalmajor* Julius Ringel, arrived at Maleme by air, despite the bombardment to which the aerodrome was continuously being subjected by the New Zealand artillery. (IWM CM880).

Meanwhile, at Heraklion, although they were evacuated from the city centre, the survivors had made a stronghold in the suburbs, from where they would no longer be expelled.

That night, a combat took place between a German convoy protected by a small destroyer, commanded by the captain of the *Regia Marina*, Francesco Mimbelli, who confronted the H.M.S. «*Orion*», preventing the entire fleet of caiques from being sunk.

22nd May 1941: The change

Four battalions of *Gebirgsjäger*, with the chief of the Division, *Generalmajor* Julius Ringel at the head, reached Maleme throughout the day. The un-aimed New Zealand artillery continued with its bombardments, but these artillery attacks remained very imprecise and hence they hardly bothered the operation in course. As soon as he arrived, *Generalmajor* Ringel assumed command and organised the advance of the troops towards Chania and Souda. He divided his forces into three Kampfgruppe. The first of them, commanded by Ramcke, had the mission of garrisoning the aerodrome and surrounding area and later advancing parallel to the coast. Another *Gruppe* headed towards Kastelli (Casteli or Kissamos), being commanded by Major Schaette. And, finally, a third *Gruppe* under the command of *Major* Utz was to carry out a flanking manoeuvre in the mountains, finally heading eastwards.

In the prison at Ayia, *Major* Derpa, commander of the II./FJR 3, sent his men to conquer the nearby high areas, which they then controlled. There was a succession of confrontations and attacks in which Greek troops and civilians from the island participated, commanded by British officers. The fight was very hard and bitter and once again, local savagery made its appearance, but this time, and in spite of their extreme exhaustion, the *Fallschirmjäger* sold their lives dearly. The action finally died out on its own, above all due to the death of the commander of the unit that momentarily stopped the Germans.

On this day, the 22nd June, the interpretation of the superior commanders, Hitler in Berlin and Student and Freyberg near the battle-

A group of *Fallschirmjäger* saying their last goodbyes to their fallen comrades. Among the graves is *Major* Derpa, commander of the II./FJR.3. (Bundesarchiv 141-0848).

field was distanced from the reality. In Berlin, the news was pessimistic and a not very rosy

The *Fallschirmjäger* maintained the runway operative at any cost and when an aeroplane was damaged, they removed it from the runway with the help of the Bren Carriers taken at the aerodrome, although in the process, they inflicted more damage on it than it had initially suffered. (Bundesarchiv 101I-166-0512-39).

Attacking Maleme with the Junkers Ju 52 also enabled the German troops to be supplied with the collective weapons and some vehicles they were capable of transporting within their fuselage, such as the motorcycles with sidecars, which were so vital for the liaison mission. The illustrations on the following page shows a DKW NZ 350 motorcycle and BMW R 75 whit sidecar. (Bundesarchiv 146-2005-0021 y 101I-543-0569-17).

outcome was expected. Student was perhaps more optimistic, but he only had one card to play: Maleme, and although this seemed to give a result, he was very worried about the fate of all the isolated groups near the other targets. Perhaps the most mistaken was Freyberg's General Staff, concretely Brigadier James Hargest, who thought that the carrousel of aeroplanes at Maleme was dedicated to evacuating the troops that had arrived previously. Freyberg was also optimistic, but not excessively. The disaster for the Germans that had been the dispersion of their first maritime convoy, which had occurred that night, had given him hope, but the stagnation and deadlock of the paratroopers' positions on the island was a bad sign if they did not manage to eliminate them.

Freyberg had remained hesitant in employing his reserve, the Battalions 18th (New Zealand), 2/7th (Australian), 23rd, 28th and the Welsh Battalion, but it was already too late and faced with the German pressure, he decided to withdraw the 5th New Zealand Infantry Brigade to new positions. Freyberg had just realised that the situation was turning against him.

CHAPTER VI
THE BATTLE CHANGES COURSE

23rd May

The 5th New Zealand Infantry Brigade received the order to attack, but only the 20th

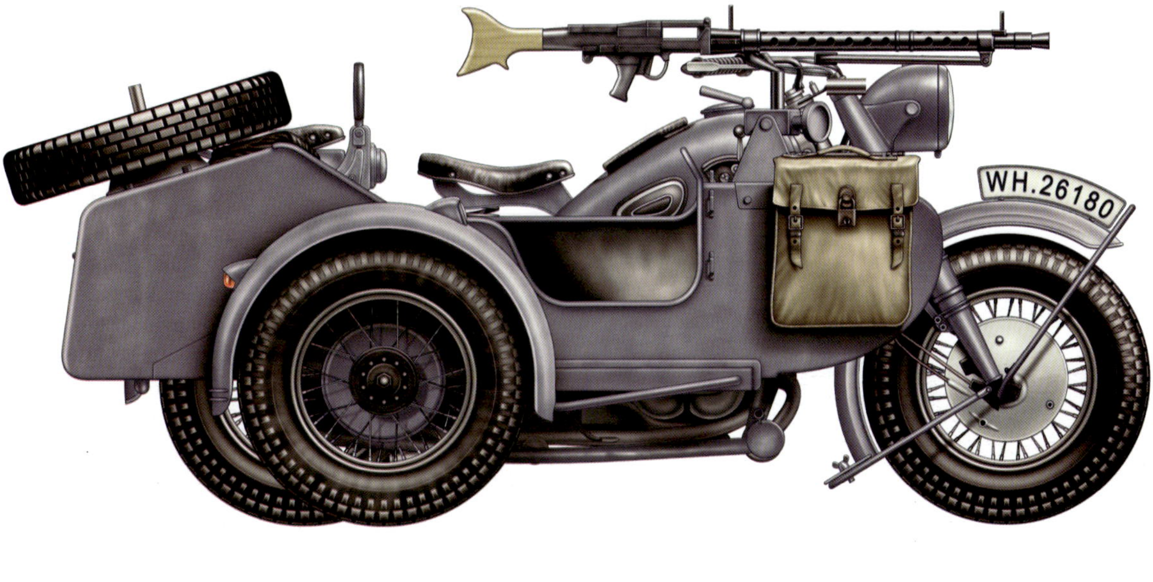

Loading onto the Junkers Ju 52/3mg a 7.5 cm *Gerbirgsgeschütz* 36 and a small half-track SdKfz 2 *kleines Kettenkraftrad*, indispensable for towing the piece of artillery through the difficult Cretan orography.

Artwork: Julio López Caeiro.

and 28th (Maori) obeyed, with the support of what was left of the 21st from their positions. Once again, the advance was fruitless and the British were forced to retreat to the starting points of their action, as a result of the success of the surprised paratroopers.

The initiative was in the hands of the Germans and they did not fail to take advantage of this. The *Gruppe Ramcke* commenced its advance parallel to the coast, for which it made use of the Bofors cannons captured at Maleme. The advance was rapid, as the retreat of the New Zealanders the previous day had left open a broad zone of no-man's-land. During their advance, at the abandoned British positions, the paratroopers found the bodies of their comrades, who had fallen prisoner to the New Zealanders on the first day, with bullets in their heads. This violation of international treaties added to many irregularities and actions that had already taken place during that attack and would make its mark the day after the conquest.

Similarly, the battalion of sappers that was heading towards Kastelli, found another 130 paratroopers from the first waves, murdered and horribly mutilated. This episode, adding to the previous, caused outrage among the German troops, who from this moment onwards, began to settle accounts with the Greek civilians, the possible caused of the butchery that did not end until several days after the final conquest. Finally, the small town was taken with its port, that is, with the help of the *Luftwaffe* supporting the action with Junkers Ju 87 Stuka. This conquest was very important, as the first port was obtained that the caiques could access with their precious cargo.

Meanwhile, the *Gruppe Utz* confronted the Greeks of the 8th Regiment near Modion. The Greeks ordered hard resistance, but the paratroopers annihilated the resistance and took the town. While advancing eastwards, they

In spite of the cannon fire to which the airfield at Maleme was subjected from artillery and ships anchored at Souda Bay, the shots were not accurate enough to hinder the operation in course.

Other material was supplied with the help of parachutes, such as the PaK 37 anti-tank cannon in this snapshot. (Bundesarchiv 141-0853).

A

Zerstörer Messerschmitt Bf 110D from the II./ZG 76, based at the aerodrome of Argos.
Artworks: Julio López Caeiro.

Pressured by the advancing *Kampfgruppe Utz*, the New Zealanders abandoned Hill 295 and the artillery positioned there, with which they had been bombing the Maleme aerodrome. Taking control of the hill provided relief from the continuous harassment to which the aerodrome had been subjected and freed from the British artillery, it became completely operative, having secured the runway. (Bundesarchiv 141-0828 y 146-1980-090-34).

clashed with the 5th New Zealand Brigade, which clearly retreating, abandoned Hill 295 and the artillery positioned there, with which they had bombed the aerodrome of Maleme. They were half fleeing, half retreating and the control of the hill provided relieve from the continuous harassment in the direction of the aerodrome, which once freed from the British artillery, became totally operative, with the runway secured from an artillery attack.

24th May.
Souda Bay

Colonel Laycock was a very particular character. He was admired, feared, though above all hated by many and landed at Souda Bay with two hundred commandos. The cruiser HMS «*Abdiel*» had transported the commandos there as reinforcements to the defenders, although with the mission of not fighting in a regular manner, but rather trying to carry out special infiltrations and counter-attacks against the elite German troops. Laycock's men arrived at a place where disaster reigned. Some of the commanders were bloody-minded and only obeyed orders rigorously and without any kind of flexibility, This, combined with the inefficiency and lack of charisma of others and their estrangement from the troops, the majority of whom were British (if not English), which were characterised for being constituted of the "sort" that needed a heavy hand in order for military discipline to function correctly, had created a less than recommendable situation in Souda and Chania. With the lamentable spectacle that they found there: Demoralised and drunk men committing all kinds of excesses, officers unconcerned about their men and a coming and going of orders and counter-orders, often broken, the commandos saw that their work was going to be very hard against the disciplined and dedicated Germans.

Fallschirmjäger photographed in the town of Chania after its occupation. (Bundesarchiv 183-B10719).

The taking of Chania

The *Fallschirmjäger* attacked following the axis of the road leading to Chania. The New Zealanders were defending the small city, in which chaos reigned in the streets. In this setting, the Germans took control, after capturing the survivors of the attack, or causing them to flee. Only British soldiers managed to retreat to the defensive line that separated Chania from Souda Bay. But the company commanded by *Hauptmann* Von der Heydte was stopped when leaving the town. For several hours, they were completely paralysed. Then they managed to break through the New Zealanders' line again and advance along the road to Souda.

25th May
The Chania road

Ringel's troops advanced eastwards in their double column and during the early hours, made contact with the *Fallschirmjäger* who were taking shelter at Ayia. Early in the morning, the Messerschmitt Bf 109 and Bf 110 attacked the Galatas zone and machinegunned the 18th New Zealand Battalion for several endless minutes. Then, the cannons with no recoil, the mountain shells of the 75th and the mortars of the 80th made a selection of targets in the British line, to later carry out the attack. The German attack was contained strongly by the New Zealanders, but they were eventually overcome. The New Zealand flank companies withdrew their lines, seeking houses in the town as a better line of defence.

The strong German pressure finally managed to disband the British, but the streets of the town were strewn with Greek refugees from nearby towns, all kinds of goods, military material and a great number of wounded who had been evacuated there in the hope of being transferred to the rearguard. All this was a barrier to and even blurred the minutely calculated tactical action that the Fallschirmjäger were conducting. Furthermore, it prevented them from making the appropriate

After taking Chania, staff Mayor *Oberst* Richard Heidrich (FJR 3) unfurling the swastika flag. (Bundesarchiv 141-0840).

reaction when elements of the 23rd New Zealand Battalion came to assist the members of the 18th, supported by Mk VI light tanks. A fight to the death ensued amid the chaos of the jammed streets. The paratroopers were exhausted from the great effort and lack of water and supplies and began to lose ground. Finally, they were obliged to leave what they had conquered in the hands of the enemy, together with the 150 German bodies fallen in the battle.

However, the British tactical victory had been useless. General Freyberg, accused by many of the inappropriate management of the operations, made another of his many unjustified manoeuvres by ordering the 23rd Battalion to retreat from the town. According to him, there was a high change that the Germans would surround it during the night and cut off the men who were defending it and he preferred to use his forces for more important purposes. At dawn, the Germans began a new attack, but they found the town abandoned; the British had disappeared together with the small crowd of Greek refugees. In the streets, there were only abandoned corpses, the remains of vehicles and smouldering rubble. Now, nobody stood in their way and the Germans understood it as such.

Rethymno

Ringel had decided that the rescue of the besieged paratroopers at Rethymno and Heraklion was the priority, even if by doing so many British would be able to escape from the island. The *esprit de corps* came before the military victory. Ringel assigned *Oberstleutenant* Wittmann, artillery commander of the *Gebirgsjäger Regiment 95* with this priority mission: Contact had to be made with them at any cost.

At Stavromenos, the *Gruppe Koch* paratroopers had dug trenches and managed to repel the various attacks that had been made on them over the past few days. On at least two occasions, they had been obliged to alter their positions, due to the exposed nature of their emplacement. The *Gruppe* commanded by Wiedemann had made a stronghold at Perivolia, three kilometres from Rethymnon. Its

situation wasn't very good, as the possibilities of its scarce components were greatly diminished, although morale was very high.

Until the 24th, their situation had been very awkward, above all, because they were isolated by the lack of operative radios, which left the unit with very few options. As a means of communication, they were only able to write messages in the sand of the nearby beach in the hope that they would be spotted by their aircraft. They were soon located by their aviation, which sent them messages by dropping them directly on them, to later commence a constant supply of more urgent logistics. The situation did not allow any other action to be taken for the time being. However, on the 24th, given that the operation on Maleme was successful, General Student decided to detract forces to assist the cornered paratroopers in the east and centre of the island.

Heraklion

The situation worsened among the isolated sections and companies that had managed to entrench themselves in concrete positions, due to the relentless sun (sun and flies, as an aviator later said), the lack of water and scarcity of ammunition complicated the resistance even further.

Their great problem, apart from being surrounded by several British units, was the Cretan guerrillas, who harassed them continuously, taking advantage of any oversight to kill and rob the wounded and then flee.

The British did not participate directly in the destruction of these small *Gruppe*, as their main effort was focused on Maleme and above all on preventing amphibious landings. Furthermore, they thought that their annihilation would occur with the passage of time, without the exposing their forces unnecessarily. Thus, for instance, they did not prevent *Major Schulz' Gruppe* from joining with that of

Photographic report from Franz Peter Weixler's camera, showing a British position being taken by the *Fallschirmjäger*, which may well have been the taking of Hill 137. (Bundisarchiv 101I-166-0508-27, 28, 31, 32, 35, 0509-06, 13, 14, 16, 17 y 0510-05).

Oberst Brauer, which improved their ability to face the upcoming actions.

During the days of waiting, thanks to the supplies received, above all in weapons and ammunition, as well as the recovery of some of the wounded who were able to carry out defensive labours, quite a lot of the most able men were made available for action. Under these circumstances, the perimeters in which they were surrounded could be enlarged in a limited, but progressive manner. Amongst other advances, they managed to take the nearby Hill 137, which left the aerodrome inoperative for the British, as the hill overlooked the main runway.

Finally, also on the 24th, two companies of *Fallschirmjäger* jumped over Heraklion and reinforced the besieged. With them, a large amount of supplies were sent, and above all water and ammunition, which was what they lacked the most. The availability of personnel on the ground enabled a perfect jump with hardly any losses, because prior to this, those who were on Crete had carried out a good job of providing information on the area and the most appropriate time for the drop. Also, and exactly when the jump was about to take place, the controlled zone was increased and the Cretan irregular soldiers were distracted with several diversion attacks.

The operation was a complete success and the reinforcements enabled new advances to be made, which were curiously facilitated by the retreat of the British, who appeared to have no interest on putting an end to the German paratroopers.

CHAPTER VII
MORALE

Freyberg was beaten. The situation on the west of the island was chaotic. The continuous abandonment of one line of defence after another did not predict anything positive. In fact, these tactical retreats were unnecessary in many cases and were merely precautionary measures, but in doing so, the troops' moral had fallen very low. The continuous retreats, when the feeling was that although the enemy was harassing them, he didn't have much chance, heavily affected the ordinary soldier, often even more so than the high ranking officers of the General Staff. As many veterans of Russia said: "*the Iron Crosses grow in the offices*" and the General Staff officers often think that the battles are fought by little flags stuck on a map, when they are actually fought fiercely

by soldiers on the battlefield, in then midst of death, with fear gripping their throats.

News from Souda

The progress of the *Gerbirgsjäger Regiment 141* was steady and remarkable. Only during the final moments and when General Freyberg unexplainably gave up the game for lost, did a violent confrontation occur with the remains of some of the Australian and New Zealand units in a last desperate attempt at containing the advance. This, combined with the attack by Colonel Laycock's irregular soldiers, slowed down rather than stopped the conquest of Souda. However, fate was already sealed.

The regular troops of the New Zealand Brigade were totally overrun, with all their battalions diminished or disappeared in the face of the German advance. The defence was really unstoppable. Under these circumstances, another 300 British commandos landed to reinforce those who had arrived forty-eight hours earlier under the command of Colonel Laycock. They had been trying to do their work, but the chaotic defence and the excellent organisation of the Germans had rendered many of their actions unfruitful. Also, the irregular Greek soldiers, who had occasionally been mistaken for Germans, had wreaked havoc in their lines. With these new reinforcements, General Freyberg hoped to gain time, because even he was aware that conquest was now inevitable, above all if, as also noted here, the Germans managed to take the ports to disembark their troops.

Retreat

In the afternoon on the 26th, Freyberg informed Wavell of the impossibility of maintaining Crete in the medium term and that furthermore, the price in losses and material would be very high if they continued to cling onto the island. From Egypt, Wavell sent his approval for an organised retreat that firstly placed as many British men as possible off the island and secondly, the Allies and civilian personnel. By then it was the 27th May.

27th May
A day of respite

Operation *«Barbarossa»* began to be prepared and reinforcements were needed at

In the afternoon of the 26th, Freyberg communicated to Wavell the impossibility of holding Crete in the medium term and furthermore that the cost in losses of men and material would be very high if they continued to cling on to the island. (IWM E3021E).

the frontier with the Soviet Union. Hitler and his OKW decided that it was time to start removing material from other fronts to reinforce the new one that would shortly arise, so the *Luftwaffe* started to remove some of the Messerschmitt Bf 109 and Bf 110 that were operating over Crete. The German command lost the eyes that were watching the British retreat and also the means with which to harass them, which combined with the strange path chosen for the British retreat, via Skafia, enormously hindered Ringel's decisions. This was a gift for General Freyberg. His approach to the retreat, full of orders and counter-orders, consisted in evacuating his troops (basically via Skafia), from the south of the island and required among other things, aerial tranquillity. And Hitler was kind enough

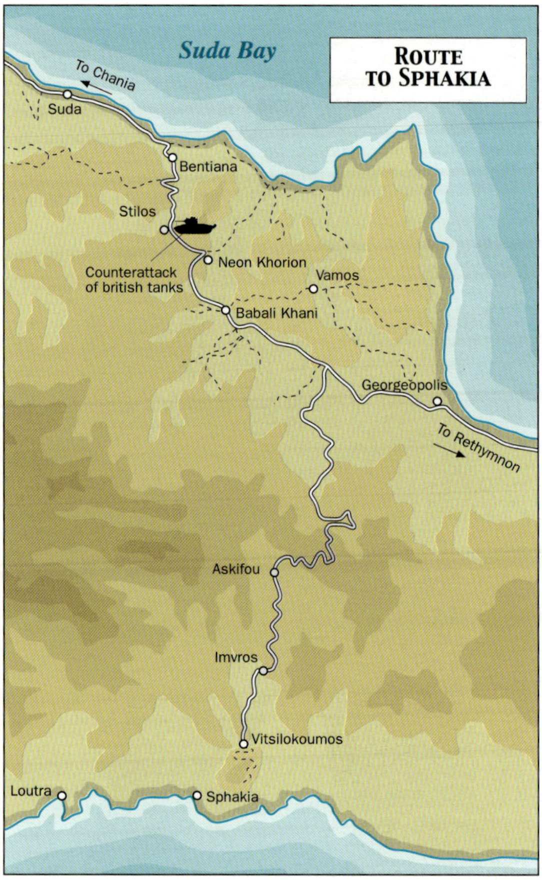

to present him with this. Nevertheless, and as had already happened in other places from the Spanish War of Independence to Dunkirk, the British troops carried out a retreat marked by chaos, lack of adequate cover to protect themselves from the German vanguard and, above all, a lack of discipline. The British officers washed their hands of their soldiers on many occasions and the soldiers committed all sorts of pillages, rapes and crimes on the Cretan population during their meander towards the south of the island. The wounded were left to their chances or the goodwill of their comrades and the means of transport were used fraudulently on many occasions for interests unrelated with the army. But once again, as we have already mentioned, luck was on their side, as General Student was more interested in saving as many of his men alive as he could, than capturing the hoard that was fleeing southwards.

Rethymo and Heraklion.

Meanwhile, in the central and eastern parts of Crete, new companies of paratroo-

On the 28th, new companies of *Fallschirmjäger* were dropped within the zones already controlled by the Germans to reinforce them and help with the expansion. (Bundesarchiv 527-2348-21 y 527-2349-04).

pers jumped within the zones already controlled by the Germans to reinforce them and assist with their expansion. The commanders of the different Gruppe were surprised at the ease with which these manoeuvres were carried out as time went by. They were unaware of the order to retreat southwards that the British units had received, which was allowing them not only to survive, but also to conquer targets that were initially considered little more than impossible, after the initial failure.

Skafia

The *Gebirgsjäger Regiment 141,* which was comprised of the vanguard of the German mountain troops, pursued the British troops southwards in their retreat, but without forcing excessively the safety distances or the confrontations with the British. Sporadically, the Australian and Maori troops made attacks to delay their progress. These actions were alternated by the 19th Australian Brigade and the 5th New Zealand Infantry Brigade. During the night, and already in broad daylight on the 28th, a strong skirmish occurred, which brought a Victoria Cross to Sergeant Hulme; it was one such action that started out as a confrontation and ended up as a small battle with many losses.

28th May

The German troops started to flank their action, seeking the south of the island. The 23rd New Zealand Infantry Battalion assisted by the tanks and artillery, tried to contain the Germans at Stilos, a crossroads between southern and eastern routes, in the interior of

During one combat, between the vanguard mountain troops and retreating British, which took place on the 28th, barely five minutes were sufficient for the PaK 37 anti-tank cannons to destroy several Vickers Mk VI light tanks and two *Matilda* Mk II infantry tanks.
Artwork: Julio López Caeiro.

the island. They had already passed the Souda Bay meridian and the route to Heraklion was open. The dirt track, that was called a road there, was quite impassable at some points, but *Gerbirgsjäger* units had already gone beyond the defences of the 23rd New Zealand Battalion and taken the Kalami Bridge in a surprise attack. At Stilos, the New Zealanders had been overcome by some Germans who had made good use of their 80 mm mortars and anti-tank cannons. They realised that the Mk VI light tanks and two Matilda were blocking their path. The fight lasted for three hours, but there were five crucial minutes during which the tanks entered into action against the Germans and they took great pleasure in destroying them.

The advance of *Kampgruppe Wittmann,* along the coastal highway and *Kampgruppe Krabau* in a flanking manoeuvre along a route through the mountains some ten kilometres from the coast was only hindered by the Layforce commandos. The German superiority was soon imposed, as the small tanks and vehicles with the no-recoil cannons supported the infantry very well. The advance was continuous and Rethymno was felt to be close. Only at Chania, already relatively close to Rethymno, there was a makeshift Allied unit blocking the road. While part of the German vanguard observed them, others

flanked and overcame them after a short battle.

Meanwhile, on the road leading southwards, the final confrontation took place between the British tanks and the mountain troops of the *Gebirgsjäger Regiment 100*, which was commanded by *Oberst* Willibald Utz. The 23rd New Zealand Infantry Battalion and three tanks managed to gain time by stopping two battalions of mountaineers. However, the end was less than forty-eight hours away. The British retreated along the meandering roads to the plain of Askifou, very close to Skafia. These roads, actually forest trails, in the middle of an arid and rocky landscape that occasionally ended in cliffs or dead ends saw the desperate flight of the troops. In the final stretch, the healthy men passed for wounded in order to be boarded as soon as possible.

When the first *Panzerkampfwagen IV Ausf D* of the *Panzer Regiment 35* (*5.Panzerdivision*) landed on the 27th May at the small port of Kastelli, the outcome of the battle had already been decided by the bold behaviour of the *Fallschirmjäger*.

Artwork: Luis Fresno Crespo.

27th May
Open path to Rethymno

The General Staff of the CREOFORCE flew southwards, planning a stopover at Skafia. The 5th and 19th Brigades received the order to retreat, not to take up positions in a new line cutting off the advance towards Heraklion, but rather to head south. Freyberg began to be in a hurry to abandon the island. Souda had been under German control for almost 48 hours and they had begun to disembark troops and above all vehicles, tanks and heavy artillery, in large quantities. In his precipitated flight, Freyberg committed the unforgivable mistake: Failing to advise Colonel Campbell, who was commanding the forces at Rethymno to retreat.

Taking Rethymno and Heraklion

The Germans advanced towards Rethymno and were hindered by Lieutenant Colonel Campbell's men at the gate. He had entrenched his forces in the hills overlooking the city and the outskirts of the airport and port. The Germans decided to wait for the arrival of armoured vehicles and 15 cm artillery, which were on their way there. When they joined them, they would attack the Australian positions. When the large calibre pieces started

The 15 cm pieces, which served to 'soften' the Australian positions at Rethymno, were *15 cm schweres Infanteriegeschütz 33*, pertaining to the *13. Kompanie* of each *Fallschirmjäger Regiment*.

Artwork: Julio López Caeiro.

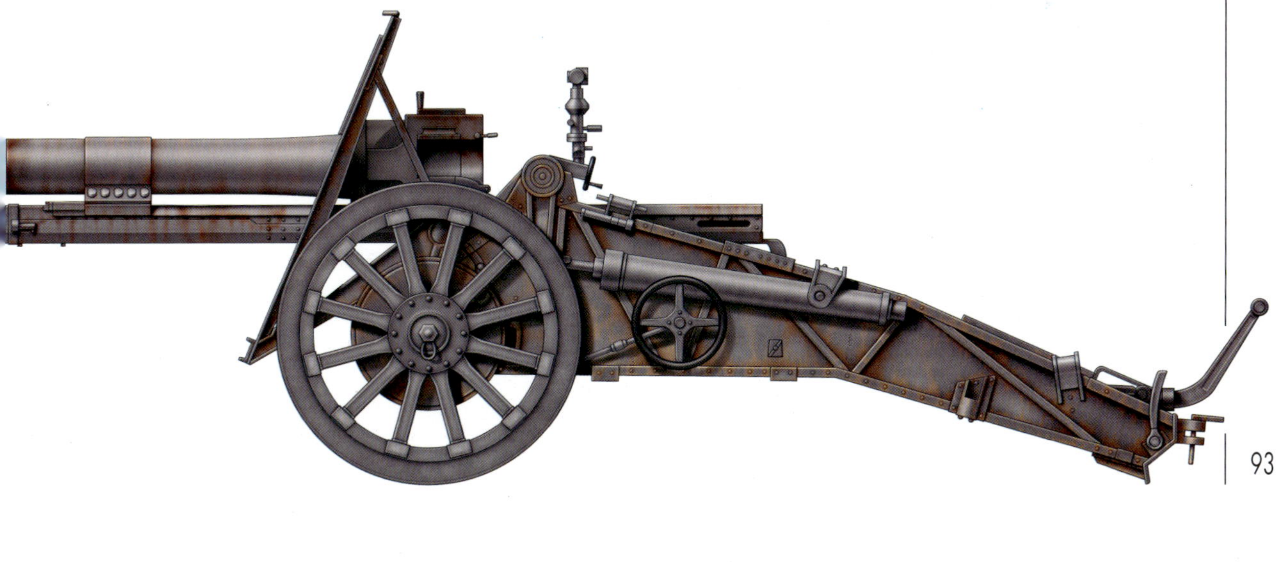

When Lieutenant Colonel Ian R. Campbell, military commander of Rethymno, asked for surrender, *Oberst* Alfred Sturm and the parachutists of the *Fallschirmjäger Regiment 2* that had been taken prisoner on the first day were freed. Contrastingly, more than seven hundred Australian soldiers went to join those taken captive on Crete, like those that we can see being treated in an improvised first-aid post in the shelter of a destroyed German plane, protected from the sun by parachute canvases. (IWM E3066E y E3135E).

In this shot, we can see the light cruiser HMS *Dido*, one of the components of the B Force, which managed to evacuate four thousand members of the Heraklion garrison on the night of the 28th to 29th, taking advantage of the darkness. However, the operation was not without repercussions, as on the way to Alexandria, the destroyer HMS *Imperial* was sunk by dive bombers and the cruiser HMS *Orion* was hit on three occasions, resulting in serious damage and numerous dead among the evacuees. The HMS *Decoy* also suffered some damage. The HMS *Hereword* and the HMS *Dido* suffered minor damage, as they were hit in the "B" tower by Junkers Ju 87 *Stuka*. (IWM FL 5208).

to beat their positions, the Australians individually began to surrender. First individual soldiers, then by sections and companies and finally, Lie utenant Colonel Campbell asked for surrender and handed over the prisoners he had taken on the first day: Oberst Alfred Sturm and the paratroopers of the *Fallschirmjäger Regiment 2*. More than 700 Australian soldiers boosted the lines of British captivity on Crete.

However, at Heraklion things turned out differently. Taking advantage of the night, 3,500 men deployed in the sector were boarded on the cruisers HMS *«Dido»* and HMS *«Orion»* and their escort of six destroyers. From the positions that they had been expanding, the surrounded paratroopers observed the movements of the British, but they thought that they were reinforcements arriving at the port. Not only did they lack control of the port, but their positions were far away from it. In the morning, they discovered that only isolated groups of Cretans remained in the surrounding area. They quickly went to liaise with the troops that were coming from Rethymno, as well as informing about the abandonment of the plaza by the British. Meanwhile, a convoy that was destined further west was deviated to Heraklion, before the men advancing along the road arrived. The convoy contained Italian troops who took the port, while the paratroopers took the abandoned city. Finally, the *Gebirgsjäger* made contact with them. Wittmann's men reached the aerodrome at nightfall, with some precautions, as there was a degree of activity inside, but they were not troops but rather Cretans, who were trying to dismantle it before the German troops arrived.

At the same time, in the Lerapetra desert, at the most south-easterly tip of Crete, an advance column took the most faraway point, within those predictable.

When they occupied the deserted Heraklion, the Germans found some barricades erected from stone in front of the west gate of the old medieval wall.

From the 29th to 31st May

More than 5,000 men were captured at Skafia, among them components of the 2nd/7th Australian Infantry Battalion. This unit, the last charged with protecting the retreat, was captured completely and its commander, Lieutenant Colonel Theo Walter, perhaps the highest ranking officer taken prisoner, as the rest had already left the island. General Freyberg personally left aboard a Short Sunderland seaplane on the 30th; his General Staff were evacuated with him.

Often, the rest of the prisoners found themselves in conditions that we have been recounting: Men who got drunk when they became aware that they would be captured and committed all kinds of abuses.

Once again, what had happened at Dunkirk was repeated, though the attitude of the troops was less military and heroic, with a few exceptions. First the wounded were evacuated, the majority of the officers and commandos of the Layforce, then the remainder continued to be evacuated without any order or arrangement. Nevertheless, climbing onto a

Lacking the majority of their organisational vehicles, the *Fallschirmjäger* used whatever British vehicles they could find in working order, such as the Morris CS8 shown in the illustration.

Artwork: Julio López Caeiro.

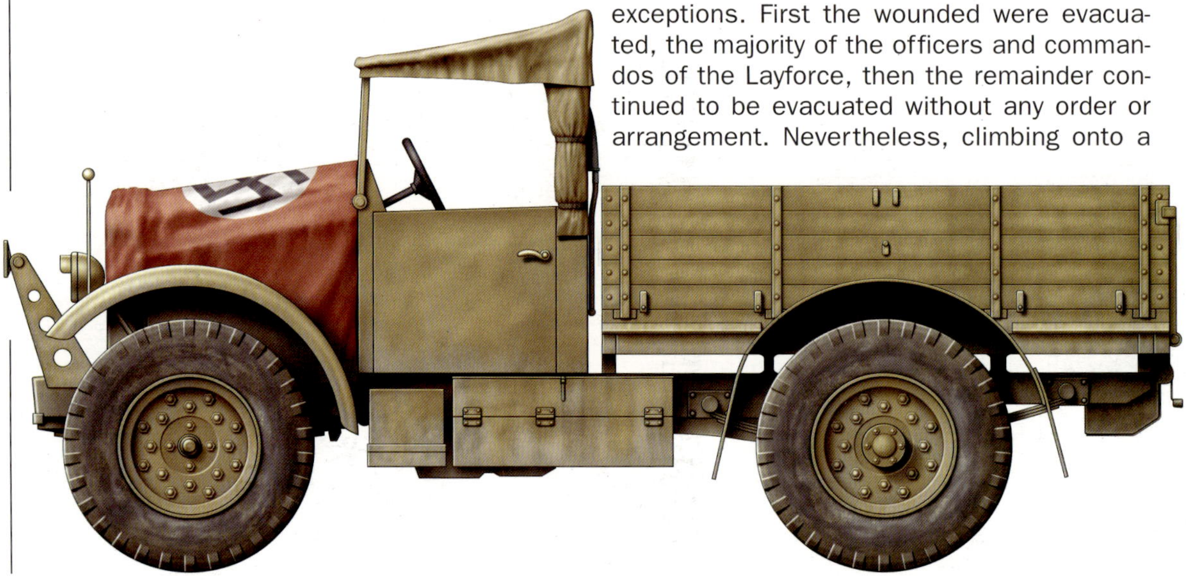

ship did not guarantee anything, as some of the ships ended up resting on the bottom of the sea with their cargo of desperate men. This was the fate of the HMS *«Calcutta»*, which was sunk by the *Luftwaffe* on the 1st June, while completely loaded and on course for Egypt.

CHAPTER VIII
SHIPS AND AEROPLANES

Within the episode of providing reinforcements to the aerial attack troops, three naval convoys were planned, which were to transport mountain troops, wheeled and chained vehicles, together with pieces of artillery that should provide the fire power necessary to conquer the island.

More than 5,000 men were captured at Skafia, among them components of the 2nd/7th Australian Infantry Battalion. This unit, the last charged with covering the retreat, was captured entirely and its chief, Lieutenant Colonel Theo Walter, perhaps the highest ranking officer, was taken prisoner, the rest having already left the island. (Bundesarchiv 183-L19113).

Between the 20th May and 1st June, the British decided to hinder as much as possible, the naval activity of the Axis forces. Despite their undeniable superiority (both naval and land-based), of which the significance of the aerial attack and later paratrooper attack were known, General Freyberg was always expecting a large amphibious landing. British Intelligence always that what was anticipated was what really happened, but the British command, on the other hand, always expected a more significant amphibious attack, which they thought would not have been detected by the Allied intelligence services.

Anticipating the convoys

Several days prior to the action, the minelayer *«Abdiel»* had already laid mines along the eastern coast of Greece in an heroic display, as the German aviation was on the lookout for any kind of British ship detected, as will be demonstrated later. This minelayer resulted in the sinking of the Italian destroyer *«Mirabello»* and two of the troop transporters, among other ships.

Meanwhile, the majority of the Mediterranean fleet (an aircraft carrier, four battleships, ten cruisers, thirty destroyers and multiple smaller units) were positioned near Crete. Most of

them were positioned outside the theoretical limit of flight autonomy of the German bombers, with the intention of attacking the convoys expected, or assisting the mass evacuation of the island of Crete. In the end, two different and continuous phases were developed, whose mid-point was the 27th May. Both phases had a high cost in terms of ships and men and as shown in the adjoining boxes, in terms of naval forces and losses. Quantifying both figures places the British squadron under question and places the German aviators and their victories at very high standards.

The convoys one by one

Three convoys of reinforcements and supplies were planned. The first convoy, formed of Italian-German units, left Pireo on the 19th May 1941. Its destination was Maleme. It consisted in twenty-five small Greek ships and was to be escorted by the Italian torpedo boat *«Sirio»*, which had to be replaced by the torpedoer *«Lupo»*, due to a breakdown. This insufficient naval protection was to be compensated for by continuous aerial coverage. It was predicted that by taking a route that would always be covered by the protective shadow of the aeroplanes deployed in the different land-based aerodromes, a degree of safety would be maintained throughout the whole journey to Maleme.

The convoy was transporting elements of the *7. Flieger-Division*, some 2,250 soldiers, including components of the *III./Gebirgsjäger Regiment 100.* These reinforcements did not include their heavy material, but this was present on the Stab convoy of the *7. Flieger-Division*, two batteries of the *I./Flak-Lher-Abteilung*, a range of spare parts and some motorcycles.

The convoy was located and attacked by the British naval forces (Force D) during the night of 21st to 22nd May. The torpedo boat «Lupo» placed itself between the two enemy ships and the small caiques trying to defend their convoy. Although the caiques dispersed immediately, the sinking of 16 of them could not be avoided. 297 men died. Others managed to be rescued by the seaplanes and torpedo launchers that collaborated first in the defence of the convoy and later with the rescue of the shipwrecked. This first convoy did not manage to anchor at Crete and the survivors returned to the continent.

A second convoy left from the port of Chalkis on the 21st May. Its destination was Heraklion and it consisted in 38 small caiques and other smaller vessels. Escorted by the Italian torpedo boat *«Sagitario»*, it was transferring 4,000 men from the *5. Gebirgsjäger Division*, without their heavy equipment, a battery of the *I./Flak-Lehr-Abteilung* and diverse logistical elements. On the 22nd May, it was intercepted by Force C of the Royal Navy, comprising three cruisers and four destroyers. It seemed inevitable that all its components would be sunk, but the intervention of the *«Sagitario»*, the rapid dispersion of the caiques and the action of the *Luftwaffe* meant that Admiral King desisted in the attack, as he later claimed, due to not having enough weapons and anti-aircraft ammunition. He didn't manage to reach Crete at the first attempt either. Other convoys were later organised from his forces.

The third convoy had a very different composition to the previous. It was exclusively comprised of Italian naval forces and it left Rhodes on the 27th May at 17:00 hours, to anchor at different ports of Crete at about 17:00 hours on the 28th May. This convoy consisted in five fishing boats, two deep-sea fishing boats, four steamships, a squadron oil tanker, two small tankers and two tug boats. Its escort was very broad and varied: The destroyer *«Crispi»*, the torpedo boats *«Libra»*, *«Lince»* and *«Lira»* and six submarines. It was transporting the Italian Infantry Division *«Regina»* with all its logistics and was curiously not intercepted by the British.

The second phase of the naval action

It took place between the 26th May and 1st June and involved the transfer to Egypt and Cyprus. On the 21st, the destroyer HMS *«Juno»* was sunk, while the cruiser HMS *«Ajax»* suffered an attack by the *Luftwaffe*. During the afternoon-night of the same day, the HMS *«Ajax»* in the company of the cruisers HMS *«Dido»* and HMS *«Orion»*, escorted by four destroyers, intercepted and attacked one of the German convoys of troops, with the known outcome. On the 22nd, an attack was made by the German aviation on three destroyers, while they were patrolling to the north and once again upon their return to Crete. In other attacks, hits were suffered by the battleship HMS *«Warspite»* and the cruisers HMS *«Naiad»* and

Royal Navy (based at Alexandria)
Admiral Sir Andrew B. Cunnigan

Force A: Admiral Rawlings
Aircraft carrier: HMS *«Formidable»*
Battleships: HMS *«Queen Elizabeth»*, HMS *«Barham»*, HMS *«Warspite»* and HMS *«Valiant»*
Destroyers: HMS *«Greyhound»* (H.21.05.41), HMS *«Griffin»*, HMS *«Havock»*, HMS *«Hero»* and HMS *«Jaguar»*

Force B:
Cruisers: HMS *«Orion»* (damaged) and HMS *«Dido»* (damaged)
Destroyers: HMS *«Decoy»*, HMS *«Hereward»* (H.29.5.41), HMS *«Hotspur»*, HMS *«Imperial»* (H.29.5.41), HMS *«Jackal»* and HMS *«Kimberley»*

Force C: Admiral King
Cruisers: HMS *«Naiad»* (damaged), HMAS *«Perth»* (damaged), HMS *«Calcuta»* (H1.06.41), HMS *«Carlisle»* (damaged 22.5.41)
Destroyers: HMS *«Kandahar»*, HMS *«Nubian»* (damaged), HMS *«Kingston»* (damaged) and HMS *«Juno»* (H.21.5.41)

Force D: Admiral I. G. Glennie
Cruisers: HMS *«Gloucester»* (H.22.5.41), HMS *«Fiji»* (H.22.5.41) and HMS *«Ajax»* (damaged)
Destroyers: HMS *«Janus«*, HMS *«Kimberley»*, HMS *«Hasty»* and HMS *«Hereward»* (H.29.5.41)

5th Fleet of destroyers: Captain Lord Louis Mounbatten
HMS *«Kelly»* (H.22.5.41), HMS *«Kashmir»* (H.22.5.41), HMS *«Kipling»* and HMS *«Kelvin»* (damaged)

10th Fleet of destroyers:
HMS *«Stuart»*, HMS *«Voyager»*, HMS *«Vendetta»*, HMS *«Vampire»* and HMS *«Defender»*

14th Fleet of destroyers: Captain P. J. Mack
HMS *«Jervis»*, HMAS *«Nizam»* (damaged) and HMS *«Ilex»*

10th Fleet MTB: 7 torpedo launchers (MTB 67, 68, 213, 214, 215, 216 and 217).

HMS *«Carlisle»*. A bombardment was also made by Junkers Ju 87 *Stuka* and Junkers Ju 88 on the light cruiser HMS *«Gloucester»*, which sank to the north-east of Crete. Three hours afterwards, the HMS *«Fiji»* was surprised by Messerschmitt Me 109 fighter bombers and they sank it to the south-west of Crete. The successive attacks on the different ships left the majority of them without any anti-aircraft ammunition. On the 23rd, the destroyer HMS *«Kelly»*, commanded by Lord Louis Mountbatten, was sunk by the aviation. Next to it, its twin HMS *«Kashmir»* was attacked. On the 24th and 25th, no significant encounters occurred. On the 26th, the aircraft carrier HMS *«Formidable»* was 'touched', the destroyer HMS *«Nubian»* was sunk and other minor ships suffered various damage. All this took place near the aerial base on the island of Scarpanto. On the 28th, by then in full evacuation, the HMS *«Ajax»* and the HMS *«Imperial»* were hit. Almost all the ships were attacked and many were damaged. On the 29th, more than 4,000 men managed to be evacuated from Heraklion. On the 30th and 31st May, they were attacked and as many as four more cruisers and several destroyers suffered damage. Finally on the 1st June, the HMS *«Calcutta»* was sunk and the crew and passengers were carried to the bottom of the sea. The losses among the marines of the Royal Navy exceeded two thousand dead.

It was a hard sacrifice for some marines, who furthermore, had not fought with the other ships, but only with the German aviation.

The Allied aviation in Crete

Standing out by their absence, the scarce machines that had been based on the island since the 19th May left to avoid being destroyed unnecessarily, as the German superiority was such that remaining there would have been an act of suicide, where they would only be knocked down or destroyed on the ground. Only the British fighters made an appearance over their aerodromes, being mistaken by their own anti-aircraft weapons which shot them all down apart from one, which managed to escape. The RAF (Royal Air Force) was absent from this battle, due to a lack of forces.

CHAPTER IX
CONCLUSIONS ON *UNTERNEHMEN «MERKUR»*.

Operation *«Mercury»* is considered to have been the first great airborne operation carried out in the history of war. Its result was a success, in so far as the planned objective was obtained. Certainly, an excessive number of losses ensued, practically a third of all the men employed. The number of losses was too high, but one learns from mistakes. Surely, if it had been a success, like Eben Emael, sooner or later, a new operation would have ended in greater butchery. It is undeniable that the operation obtained its objective, Crete, and absolutely all those who have analysed it afterwards have drawn some conclusions from it. New operations surged from it and also new problems were thrown in to be resolved. The only truth is that had it been the tremendous failure that some accuse it of being, firstly, the objective would not have been attained and in the second place, such an operation would never have been repeated. In fact, from that moment onwards, the Allies practiced and practiced until they refined these actions, until they softening the high losses of airborne operations. Today, more than 65 years later, the paratroopers are considered to be the elite of any army.

It was something new, like almost everything the Germans did during the war. Innovation and novelty presided in any action and this kept the war machine going and kept Germany in action, until it became impossible to fight against everything and everybody.

Airborne action

The reasoning of Student and his officers was simply great, but they had forgotten that they were not just dealing with manoeuvres and that before them was a good army, the British. The almost perfect execution of the operation with the means available at the time was very well achieved, but information about the enemy and his defences was lacking, which denoted either the inexistence of German military intelligence, or overconfidence. A security failure permitted the Allies to discover the German codes and hence, through their communications, discover their plans in advance, as well as managing to get a copy of the operations order, which fell into British hands several days before the start of the operation. This helped to perfectly counteract the German approach and more importantly, neutralise the element of surprise.

On the other hand, perfect synchronisation is important in any aerial attack. This failed, due to the poor communications. It is always easy to lay the blame on radio equipment, for example, but in this case, this is what really happened: Although better means of communication that those used could have been provided.

The different proportion of the troops

The end of the Second World War instilled the theory that for each defender, there should be three attackers; this was not taken into account in the operation. Only 8,000 Germans attacked Crete in the initial plan, increasing to 23,000 by the end of the operation. On the other side, some 42,000 British were defending it. Hence they numbers were in their favour, as well as being already established in their positions. Definitively, a ratio of one to four at the start of the attack is the opposite of that considered necessary.

Student's decisions during the first hours.

The main factor was the flexibility of the Germans at all levels of their command, from General Student to the last soldier. Student was able to adapt his plan to the disaster that occurred on the first day of the attack. He was able to make decisions that involved everybody and everything to resolve the problems and win the battle. Also, and much to his credit, he preferred to save the lives of the men who were isolated and compromised in difficult situations than to capture a greater number of British prisoners, which honours him as a commander and comrade of his men. Throughout the war, no British general was the slightest bit concerned for his men and had no qualms about sending them to the slaughterhouse without any kind of worry. Marshal Montgomery is perhaps the best example of this, the worthy successor to Wellington and the purest style of the classes within the British Army.

With respect to the ethical and moral behaviour of the troops, the British attitude of permitting, even perpetrating acts on civilians that violated international conventions is incomprehensible. They broke the conventions in all manner of ways: Robbery, murder, humiliation, etc., were daily occurrences against the paratroopers who surrendered or were wounded. Afterward, this led to revenge, which was neither very fitting of the Germans and this was highly criticised by the British.

The Commonwealth

They did not reach the standards that could be expected of them; neither did their generals. Despite their great numerical superiority, they were incapable of conducting an efficient defence. Furthermore, they retreated from combat on the majority of occasions, without showing much interest in it. Their other Achilles heel, their lack of flexibility, was shown on many occasions and was one of the triggers of the failure. Orders were given and carried out according to the plan, regardless of whether the situation in the battlefield had changed; this was of no importance. In this perspective, it is easy to deduce why they lost.

Perhaps knowing the German plans beforehand facilitated the aforementioned, or not, but it is incomprehensible that knowing what the enemy was going to do, they acted as they did.

Finally, the chain of command met with all kinds of obstacles to carrying out its function. They only had themselves to blame, as all the mistakes were precisely made in the poor action of those responsible for the approaches and above all the corresponding tactical development.

Hill 107 and the centres of resistance

The actions of the Allies are impossible to understand. The New Zealanders abandoned Hill 107 overlooking Maleme, leaving the place that was an observatory and lookout, without any kind of concern, leaving one of their targets in the hands of the Germans.

It is also incomprehensible how they allowed small groups of paratroopers to entrench themselves in different places, later liaising with each other and maintaining the defence for days on end, until they were rescued by the troops that landed at Maleme.

One cannot understand the number of times the Germans were forgiven for their inferiority and allowed to recover and dig trenches awaiting better times. Finally, it is clear that the Germans won because of their initiative and that in the outcome of the operation, in view of the prism of the years gone by since 1941, the Germans did a good job. The lessons learnt were also excellent.

Lessons learnt from *Unternehmen «Merkur».*

Contrary to popular belief, Crete was a success, admittedly at a very high price, but it was a German success. It was also an inexplicable British failure, although perhaps this was due to

The behaviour of the Cretans was abominable, breaking international conventions and committing all sorts of crimes such as robbery, murder, humiliation, etc., against the surrendering German paratroopers and later resulted in the highly undignified and very violent revenge of some brave elite fighters. In the documentary collection of the Bundesarchiv in Koblenz, there is a photographic report, filmed by the reporter Franz Peter Weixler's camera, dated the 2nd June 1941, which reflects the following: The German troops arrived at a village (in which we suppose the atrocities were committed against the *Fallschirmjäger* who surrendered), they arrested the entire population,

separated the women, children and the elderly and took them outside the small village. A firing squad was formed and after placing the prisoners underneath some trees, the official order to open fire against the Cretan civilians was given. (Bundesarchiv 146-1979-125-29, 166-0525-07, 22, 25, 20, 19, 18, 28, 26, 29, 39, 30 y 527-03a).

Scene of the combats that took place in Crete in May 1941. (Bundesarchiv 141-0823).

the lack of implication by the British military command. General Wavell was more concerned about the African front, Cyprus and his ongoing conflict with his political commander, the British Prime Minister, Mr. Churchill.

Neither is it clear why the Royal Navy with an overwhelming naval superiority was incapable of containing the arrival of reinforcements that reached the island in four godforsaken fishing boats. Admiral Cunningham's inactivity and incompetence were embarrassing. He was another archetype of the British officer found at astronomical distances from the men he commanded and found anchored in the most ferocious and antiquated resistance to change.

On the other side, Hitler managed to obtain his southern flank in Greece and thus prevent the Allied actions on the oilfields and refineries of Rumania, which was his great concern. Perhaps he should have continued his action towards the Suez Canal. We will never know what would have happened if he had closed the exit from the Mediterranean there.

Hitler misunderstood the military lessons that could be extracted from this military

The human losses suffered by the German Army during the taking of Crete were very high. The *Fallschirmjäger* had 1,520 dead, 1,502 missing and more than 1,500 wounded. Without counting the losses in the convoy destroyed in the night of 21st to 22nd May, the *Gerbirgsjäger* had 395 dead, 257 missing and 504 wounded. The flight personnel suffered 85 dead, 236 missing and 127 wounded. The most noteworthy and strangest thing was the high number of missing soldiers in an army that became master of the terrain after the battle. The number of twenty doctors and medical personnel killed was also very high. In this snapshot, we can see the world heavyweight champion boxer Max Schmeling, in the hospital at Athens. Schmeling, who bore the rank of *Gefreiter*, was one of the numerous F*allschirmjäger* wounded in Crete. The photo was taken by P.K. Kassmann-Weltbild on the 6th June 1941. (Bundesarchiv 146-2006-0202).

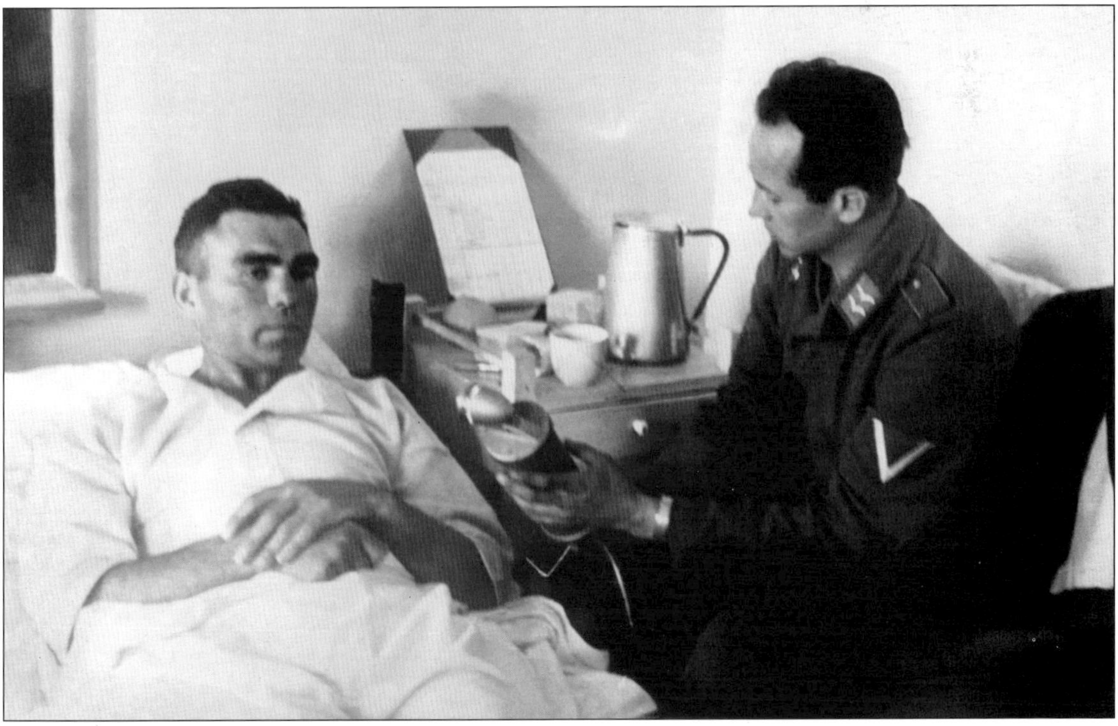

The two sides of the battle. On the obverse, it was time for laurels, rewards and medals for the victorious heroes. In the upper photo, *Oberst* Bernhard-Hermann Ramcke inspects a company of *Fallschirmjäger*, who were to be decorated. In the lower photo, the Iron Cross is being awarded to three paratroopers who displayed exceptional conduct in the battle. The scene took place on the Maleme airfield. (Bundesarchiv 101I-166-0521-12 y 0526-30).

The reverse: The bitter defeat. British and Commonwealth prisoners before being transported to concentration camps on the continent. After the battle for Crete, a total of 11,370 soldiers fell into the hands of the Germans (6,576 British, 3,102 Australians and 1,962 New Zealanders. (Bundesarchiv 101I-166-0512-12 y 183-L26106).

The *Luftwaffe's* material losses were also high, but did not reach the catastrophic levels indicated by some authors. The *VIII. Fliegerkorps* had to retire from service 52 fighters (Messerschmitt Bf 109 and Bf 110), 18 Junkers Ju 87 Stuka dive bombers, 26 twin-engine bombers and four reconnaissance planes. To these figures, one must add the some 120 triple-engine Junkers Ju 52/3mg transporters lost by the *XI. Fliegerkorps* some 120 triple-engine Junkers Ju 52/3mg transporters. (Bundesarchiv 183-B10713).

action. He was unable to see that in spite of everything, it was a success and above all, that the high cost of the operation was due to inherent factors of the still small weaponry of the paratroopers, which precisely needed to progress. The great lesson is that the paratroopers could not go so poorly armed, with just a pistol and some hand grenades, which placed them at a great disadvantage, if their other weapon of surprise failed.

The other great problem noted by many authors of the loss of transport aeroplanes during the attack, doesn't make much sense. It is comparable with the much boasted loss of men at Stalingrad. Certainly, many of the men who were captured at Stalingrad were lost and many transport aeroplanes were lost at Crete, but other operations have suffered much greater losses in one sense or another and nobody talks about them. It is simply a trend that somebody starts and the rest follow like sheep.

The Allies were able to draw the best lessons from the attack of Crete, especially the Americans. Many airborne operations took place in the Pacific and later in the Mediterranean and Normandy, with great success. Only Operation «Market Garden»*, in Holland in 1944, was a to*tal failure, but the reason was leaving its organisation in the hands of "Monty", the 20th Century Wellington and who like his predecessor, had no concern for the lives of his soldiers. His lack of interest in his men's safety and disrespect for the Intelligence reports would put an end to the lives of about forty thousand men.

Definitively, the author believes that Crete was a success for the Germans and a discredit for the British and particularly their commanders. Also, though not in a special way, we should study the attitude of Major General Bernard Cyril Freyberg, future first Baron of Freyberg, who for many years carried the blame and accusing finger of being responsible for the defeat. However, it is highly likely that he was a scapegoat for the orders received from the commanders occupying higher positions. In conclusion, we should never forget that Crete was the graveyard of the German paratroopers for the simple reason that they gave everything to win the battle and they deserve a place among the heroes of Olympus.